History, People and Places

in

HAMPSHIRE

The Square, Winchester

History, People and Places

in

HAMPSHIRE

D. M. & R. L. P. JOWITT

SPURBOOKS LIMITED

PUBLISHED BY
SPURBOOKS LTD
6 PARADE COURT
BOURNE END
BUCKINGHAMSHIRE

ISBN 0 902875 93 0

MADE AND PRINTED IN GREAT BRITAIN BY
THE GARDEN CITY PRESS LIMITED
LETCHWORTH, HERTFORDSHIRE SG6 1JS

Contents

Illustrations

Portraits of Palmerston, Charlotte Yonge and Cobbett are reproduced by permission of the National Portrait Gallery. St. Michael's Abbey Church, Farnborough is reproduced by permission of Farnborough Abbey. The Statue of the Duke of Wellington at Aldershot is reproduced by permission of Eagle Photos, Cheltenham. All other photographs are by Robert E. Jowitt.

Introduction

Even as this book is being written, the boundaries of the old Hampshire are changing. From April 1974, Bournemouth and Christchurch have been added to Dorset, under the reorganisation of local government.

Thankfully, in England it takes more than a government decree, or a line on a map, to change the history, the outlook, or the people of the old Shires, and Hampshire folk, whatever their postal address, will be Hampshire folk for many years to come.

CHAPTER I

West Hampshire

Hampshire, within the old boundaries, goes back to very ancient times, and we might well commence this history by looking at Hengistbury. The name Hengistbury comes from 'Hednesburia' or 'Hynesbury' and has no connection with Hengist.

After the last Ice Age, the ice gradually receded northward and Hampshire was one of the first habitable parts of England. Hengistbury Head, a hilly headland defended naturally on three sides by the sea, and the estuary of the Avon and Stour which join in Christchurch harbour, was probably one of the first inhabited places. Man existed in the neighbourhood even in the Old Stone Age, between the glacial periods.

About 9000 B.C., a tribe of reindeer hunters camped there, making tools from flint and reindeer antlers. Between 7000 B.C. and 3000 B.C., Mesolithic men, who could hunt with bows and arrows, and fish with harpoons, lived there. In the New Stone Age, 3300 B.C.–1500 B.C., the people were far more advanced. They kept cattle and sheep, grew wheat, and traded with Cornwall, Wales and Gaul to obtain stronger stone for their implements. There are Round Barrows, or burial mounds, from the Bronze Age, c. 1500 B.C.–500 B.C., and in them were found urns with cremated ashes, and bits of bronze and amber ornaments.

The Iron Age people, c. 500 B.C.–A.D. 400, lived in settlements of round huts with a central hearth, and they made pottery, wove cloth, made coins and had an extensive trade. They protected the landward side of Hengistbury Head by double dykes, with a wooden stockade along the top, and fought with spears, swords and slings. Even a snaffle-bit for a war-chariot horse has been found at Hengistbury. The Celts occupied the Head at one time, and a few Roman coins have been found there, the latest being of the Emperor Galleus, A.D. 351–354. Occasionally relics from the prehistoric age may still be picked up, and many from all ages may be seen in the Red House Museum at Christchurch.

After the Romans withdrew from Britain, Hengistbury Head

ceased to be occupied. It was granted to Christchurch Priory in the twelfth century. After many abortive schemes for its 'improvement' during the centuries, including a plan by Gordon Selfridge to turn it into a sort of Carcassonne, it was bought by Bournemouth Corporation in 1930. Now it has beach châlets near the Harbour Mouth, and a 'Noddy Train' to convey people to them. It is, however, an interesting place for flora and fauna, and it is only necessary to go a little off the beaten track, out of the holiday season, to forget our modern neighbours and to picture our early ancestors there.

About a mile inland from Hengistbury is Christchurch, situated on a beautiful harbour. A Saxon chronicler recorded that Twyneham, as it was then called, was captured by Ethelwold from Edward the Elder about A.D. 900. Already at that time there was a Minster Church, known as Christchurch, and this, in due course, gave its name to the town.

A legend of the church is that the original builders started to build it on a hilltop nearby, but every night the work was destroyed, and the beams were found to be too short. When the work was done again on the present site, an unknown worker, believed to have been Christ the Carpenter, lengthened the beams and the work prospered. A supposed lengthened beam is still to be seen.

William Rufus granted the town and church to Ranulph Flambard, who suppressed many of the canonries of the church, but built the

Hengistbury Head seen from near Christchurch

very beautiful Norman nave which still exists. Henry I granted church and town to a cousin, Richard de Redvers, who treated them well. In 1150 the church became a Priory of Augustinian Canons, and remained so for nearly four centuries, until the Dissolution, when it was brought to an end. Most of the monastic buildings were destroyed, but the churchwardens and parishioners were allowed to keep the church. The last Prior, John Draper, was granted a pension and a lodging. He had friends at court, and also a very good reputation in the town.

The Priory Church has a beautiful thirteenth-century porch. Norman work in the church includes the north transept, an apsidal chapel on the east of the south transept, and crypts under both transepts. The aisle and clerestory windows are thirteenth century, as are two chapels off the north transept, and some choir-stalls and quaintly-carved misericords. The west tower is Perpendicular, built instead of a former central tower, believed to have fallen in the fifteenth century. The carved rood-screen, restored in 1849, retains some fourteenth-century work, including the Adoration of the Magi, and Jesse with David and Solomon. The beautiful Salisbury Chantry, north of the altar, commemorates Margaret Pole, Countess of Salisbury, but her body was never placed there as she was beheaded in 1541 by order of Henry VIII.

There are many interesting monuments, including one fine alabaster to Sir John and Lady Chydioke, 1455, and, under the tower, one of white marble to Shelley. This had been refused by Westminster Abbey, partly because it closely resembled a 'Pietà', and partly because of Shelley's doubtful religious views, but his son gave it to Christchurch Priory when he was living at Boscombe. Underneath is the verse from Shelley's 'Adonais', beginning, 'he has outsoared the shadow of our night'. On the exterior east angle of the north transept is a richly-decorated circular turret, a very fine and interesting specimen of Norman architecture.

On the bank of the Avon in Castle Street, there is a Norman house, called the Constable's House, one of the best examples of Norman domestic architecture in this country. It is 67 feet long by 23 feet wide, with loopholes in the ground-floor walls. Part of the stone staircase to the upper floor still remains. There is also a fine chimney, and one of the upper windows has a Purbeck marble shaft, the earliest known use of this stone in England. Nearby are the remains of a Castle, consisting mainly of a keep on an artificial mound, probably built by Baldwin de Redvers in the early twelfth century, but 'slighted' by the Roundheads in 1651. The group formed by the Constable's House, Castle Keep, and the Priory

Norman Turret at Christchurch Priory

Christchurch Priory, the Constable's house and the Castle Keep

Church with its Norman turret, is a view that no lover of the Norman should miss.

Christchurch also has a six-arched medieval bridge over the Avon, several charming old houses, the very interesting Red House Museum and an excellent harbour for yachting and fishing.

Who would imagine, seeing Bournemouth now, stretching from Christchurch on the east to Poole on the west, that 200 years ago it possessed not a single house? 'La Bournemowthe' was mentioned in a Christchurch Cartulary of 1407, but this was just the mouth of the Bourne stream. In 1574 it was noted as a 'daungerous landing-place' and 'a place very easy for the ennemye to lande...being voyde of all inhabiting'. In the seventeenth and eighteenth centuries it was a great centre for smuggling, the most noted smuggler being 'Old Gulliver', who is said on one occasion to have landed three whole loads of contraband on Bourne Mouth beach.

A little inn, the Tapps Arms later to become the Tregonwell Arms, was built in what is now Old Christchurch Road, near the Square, in 1809, and in 1810 a Captain Tregonwell, who had taken a fancy to the district when he was there on military duty with the Dorset Rangers, built himself a house in what is now Exeter Road. The Exeter Hotel now stands on the spot, and the Tregonwell house is incorporated in it and marked with a plaque. From this time, the seaside resort of Bournemouth grew up at record speed. Charming villas were built on the sandy cliffs and among the pine trees, and gradually all the amenities of a resort, shops, bathing-machines, piers and concert-halls were added. Unfortunately, most of the villas have now given way to modern hotels and blocks of flats, but the Russell-Cotes Museum and Art Gallery on the East Cliff, formerly East Cliff Hall, presented to the borough by Mr. and Mrs. Merton Russell-Cotes, gives a good idea of their appearance. Many excellent Gothic Revival Churches were built, the most interesting St. Peter's by Street, architect of the London Law Courts, and St. Stephen's by Pearson, who designed Truro Cathedral.

Many literary people were associated with Bournemouth; Robert Louis Stevenson lived for a time at 'Skerryvore' near Alum Chine, and there wrote *Kidnapped, Dr. Jekyll and Mr. Hyde* and *A Child's Garden of Verse*. The house was damaged in the bombing of 1940, and had to be demolished, but a memorial garden has been made in its place.

The Chines, deep tree-clad valleys leading down to the sea, form a charming feature of Bournemouth and the sandy beaches, with beautiful views from the cliffs over the Bay to the Isle of Wight in the east and Purbeck in the west, making it one of the most attractive seaside resorts.

North of Bournemouth and Christchurch, and just west of the New Forest, is the thriving and pretty market town of Ringwood. From Bournemouth it is approached by a modern road through heath country, and from Christchurch up the Avon Valley. The latter road passes through the village of Sopley, which has a thirteenth-century church, beautifully situated on a mound above the Avon. The church stands a little way back from the road, and has interesting tombs and other features, including, on the outside supporting the north transept gable, some corbels which would certainly not have been allowed on a Victorian church. Two miles farther on is Tyrrel's Ford, where Sir Walter Tyrrel, whose arrow killed William Rufus, crossed the Avon to make his escape to France from Poole. The forge at Avon Tyrrel is supposed to be on the site of one where his horse was shod, and on this account, the smiths had to pay a yearly toll of 2s. 6d. to the Crown until the beginning of the nineteenth century.

On the way into Ringwood, No. 44 Christchurch Road is a fine eighteenth-century building, at present an Antique Shop, with two ships' figure-heads in front. Some of the shops retain their Georgian bow-windows. There is a Unitarian Chapel, 1727, with the original furnishings, in Meeting House Lane, and some pretty thatched cottages in West Street. Monmouth House, also in West Street,

Boscombe, Bournemouth in Winter

commemorates the fact that the unfortunate and misguided Duke of Monmouth was imprisoned here after his defeat at Sedgemoor in 1685. From there he wrote to his uncle, James II, begging mercy for having rebelled against him but, as might be expected, the request was not granted, and in due course Monmouth was beheaded on Tower Hill.

In the market place, a picturesque market is still held on Wednesdays. The church is a good example of Victorian Gothic, and it contains a magnificent brass, in the chancel floor, to John Prophete, d. 1416, in ecclesiastical vestments. John Prophete was at various times Dean of Hereford and of York.

About two miles north of Ringwood, and a mile east of the Salisbury road, is Moyle's Court, a Jacobean house, now a girls' school, where Dame Alice Lisle kindly, but misguidedly, sheltered some fugitives from Sedgemoor. She was arrested and taken to Winchester, and sentenced by Judge Jeffreys to be burnt to death for treason. This sentence shocked some of James II's most ardent supporters, and he commuted it to beheading, which fate the seventy-year-old lady met most courageously, on 2nd September 1685. She was buried at Ellingham, a very interesting old church near by, but her tombstone says nothing about how she met her death.

A little farther up the Avon valley, at Ibsley, there is a 'cruck cottage', a very picturesque thatched and timbered house, 'Old Beams',

A flood in the Avon valley, near Christchurch

at present a restaurant, and almost opposite it is a beautiful bridge leading to villages west of the Avon. Further on is Fordingbridge. A lovely, seven-arched medieval bridge leads into Fordingbridge, and there are some charming old inns on the north bank of the river. There was an old custom that the bridge must be guarded for fifteen nights before and after Midsummer day to prevent deer-stealers from leaving the New Forest at that point. On the south bank of the river, in the recreation ground, is a statue of the famous artist, Augustus John, who was one of the most notable inhabitants of Fordingbridge.

The church, of several styles, has many interesting features, including a beautiful Angel Roof in the north chapel. It lies to the west of the town. In Salisbury Street is the seventeenth-century Old Manor, formerly a Court House. It was owned in the present century by Mr. Morley Hewitt, an architect. He discovered, and is now excavating, a wonderful Roman villa at Rockbourne, near Sandleheath, west of Fordingbridge. It has fifty or more rooms, and includes bathrooms, mosaic pavements, and all kinds of interesting relics of the Romans, who probably lived there from the second century A.D. until they left Britain in the early fifth century.

The village of Rockbourne has many charming houses and cottages. There is a stream along the side of the main street, and the road is frequently occupied by families of fascinating ducks. The church, partly twelfth and partly thirteenth century, with some nineteenth-

Ringwood

The River Avon at Fordingbridge

Breamore Church

Breamore House

century additions and alterations, lies to the east of the village. Near by are the remains of an Elizabethan Manor House and a thirteeenth-century chapel, and a fine, late fourteenth-century barn.

About two miles north of Fordingbridge and east of Rockbourne is Breamore, pronounced Bremmer, which has a noteworthy Saxon church. Besides Saxon 'long-and-short work', it has a Saxon rood, unfortunately defaced, over the south porch, and a Saxon inscription, in letters 6 inches high, over the arch of the south transept. In translation it reads, 'Here is manifested the Word (or possibly the Covenant) to three'. Part of the church is Norman and part Perpendicular. On the Perpendicular capitals of the chancel there are beautiful carvings of natural foliage, and above the arch are the Royal Arms, including those of France and Hanover.

Breamore House, seat of the Hulse family for over 200 years, was a beautiful Tudor building. At one time it was given by Henry VIII to his fifth wife, Catherine Howard, whom he later had beheaded. It was destroyed by fire in 1853, but excellently restored in its former style. Fortunately the fine collection of works of art was largely saved. It is open to the public from 1st April to 30th September, 2 p.m. to 5.30 p.m., on Tuesday, Wednesday, Thursday, Saturday, Sunday and public holidays. In the grounds are a very interesting Agricultural Museum and a Carriage Museum. To the north-west, on Breamore Down, there is a circular 'miz-maze' of unknown date, cut out in the turf. Farther to the north-west is Grim's Dyke, where our ancestors in what is now Hampshire defended themselves against the tribes of what is now Wiltshire.

CHAPTER II

The New Forest

Returning from Breamore, cross the Salisbury road and go eastward, through Woodgreen and Godshill, into the New Forest, one of Hampshire's greatest natural glories. Woodgreen Village Hall has some very interesting murals, with portraits of the people of the village and their occupations in the 1930s. Godshill is a pretty village with thatched cottages. This is the north-west corner of the Forest, where the Avon forms the Forest boundary for a little way. Near Godshill is Castle Hill, a wooded bluff with possibly Norman earthworks. From it there is a glorious view over the Avon valley. A mile farther south is a large British camp.

Far from being 'New,' the Forest is now known to have been inhabited as long ago as the Old Stone Age. Before the time of King Canute, all wild beasts and birds in the kingdom were royal perquisites. Canute, who was, on the whole, a sensible king, moderated the law so that landowners were allowed to hunt and kill the wild birds and animals on their own land, but the Crown still had the right to 'afforest' any land. The legend was spread by the Saxons, who hated the Normans, that William the Conqueror 'made' the New Forest, destroying villages and churches, rendering whole populations homeless in the process, and spoiling valuable agricultural land. What he actually did was to declare the area a Royal Hunting Ground, and to put it under a new code of Forest Laws: hence its name, the 'New Forest', though it had in fact existed for thousands of years, part of it being tree-covered, and part open heath-land, very little of the land being suited to agriculture.

The Normans were passionately devoted to hunting, and anything which interfered with it in any way was subject to very severe penalties. The beasts and birds which were then hunted in the Forest were the buck, doe, roe, fox, marten cat, which no longer exists in the Forest, hare, rabbit, pheasant and partridge. People could be fined, blinded, lose a hand or even their lives for hunting any of these creatures, the punishments varying according to the rank of the offender, the lower the rank, the higher the penalty. The New Forest people had, however, various privileges to compensate for their losses over hunting. They were allowed 'estovers' or wood fuel, 'turbary' or turf fuel, marl for dressing the land, bracken for bedding, and 'rights of pasture', under which cattle, sheep and horses could be turned out on to the open waste lands of the King's Forest, and 'pannage', or turning out of pigs at certain times, from 25th September until 22nd November, when the acorns and beech-mast are on the ground. These rights are still held by Forest commoners, and one of the most charming sights of the Forest is the animals wandering about at will, especially the ponies with their foals. The wild animals are not so often seen now, though there is always a chance of seeing the deer.

A curious fact about the Forest Rights was that they belonged not to the owner of the property, but to the hearthstone or fireplace of a house or cottage. Sometimes the owner of a house, even if he moved or pulled the house down, would leave the fireplace standing in order to keep the rights, so that one occasionally sees a fireplace standing by itself, perhaps in the middle of a cabbage-bed, serving no apparent purpose. There was also a law or custom, called 'Keyhold Tenure', whereby if a man could build a hut in a single night so that the fire could be alight in the hearth the next morning, the hut and adjoining plot of land became his in perpetuity. In a few places, mushroom villages sprang up in this way, but the custom came to an end by about the end of the eighteenth century.

Woodgreen Mill on the Avon

The northern part of the Forest consists mainly of open heath and bracken-covered moorland, with high-standing ridges, from which there are glorious views, divided by 'bottoms' with streams running into the Avon. On one of the highest places formerly stood Bramshaw Telegraph, one of a chain of semaphore signals for sending messages from Plymouth to London. Another line of these telegraph stations connected London and Portsmouth, and a message could be sent in less than a minute. They were in use from about 1795 until 1847. Some of the timber from Bramshaw Wood was used in the building of Salisbury Cathedral. The first turning to the right after Bramshaw Telegraph leads to the pretty village of Fritham, and a track from this village leads to Sloden, one of the very old woods of the Forest, with oak, ash, whitebeam, holly, thorn and particularly notable yews.

In Sloden Inclosure, the remains of many Roman pottery kilns were excavated by Mr. Heywood Sumner, one of the great authorities on the Forest. The kilns were made of puddled clay. The 'New Forest Ware' was known throughout Britain. It was turned on a wheel, and was hard, giving attractive shapes and decorations. It was made until about A.D. 350. There were potteries also in other parts of the Forest, some of them making finer ware. A path from Sloden Inclosure leads across the Dockens Water Stream to Holly Hatch Inclosure, a nineteenth-century wood, and just east of this is Anses Wood, which has some of the most beautiful beeches of the Forest, with the stream running by them.

South of Fritham on the A31 road is Stoney Cross, and about a mile eastward from this, and north of the road, is the Rufus Stone, now enclosed in iron to preserve it. The Stone is said to mark the site of the oak tree from which Sir Walter Tyrrel's arrow glanced off and killed William Rufus, on 2nd August 1100, though some modern historians prefer another site. There was some suspicion that the shot was not accidental, as William Rufus was extremely unpopular. Nothing could ever be proved, but Tyrrel was probably well advised to leave the country. William's body was taken to Winchester by a man named Purkis, whose descendants are still in the Forest.

South of the A31 is the charming little village of Minstead. It has an inn with the sign of the 'Trusty Servant' of Winchester College, and along a lane from the inn is a fascinating church, with a Saxon, or perhaps very early Norman, font, and a thirteenth-century doorway and chancel arch. More remarkable are its eighteenth-century fittings, a three-decker pulpit, two galleries, one perhaps for the musicians when churches had a small band instead of an organ, and two box pews, with separate entrances from outside, for the squire

The Rufus Stone
(New Forest)

and other gentry. One pew has its own fireplace. Conan Doyle's grave is in the churchyard, and another interesting grave is that of Thomas Maynard, a bandsman of the Hampshire Yeomanry, d. 1807, with a 'serpent' (an old musical instrument, not one of the New Forest reptiles) carved on the headstone.

Lyndhurst, farther south, is the next place of sepcial interest after Minstead. It is the capital of the Forest. It has several one-way streets, and motorists find that they have to turn east and then south to approach the west, where the church and 'Queen's House' stand. Lyndhurst was a Royal Manor at least as long ago as A.D. 980, when Elfrida, a Saxon Queen, presented it to the Abbey of Amesbury in Wiltshire. The Queen's House, or King's House when a king is on the throne, was first built about A.D. 1300. It has been much altered and enlarged during the years. Part of it is Tudor and part Stuart. It was a Royal Residence for several centuries. The last monarch to occupy it was George III, on his way to Weymouth to convalesce after his illness. Fanny Burney, who was in the Royal party as Lady-in-Waiting to the Queen, gives a delightful account of the visit in her diary. 'Carriages of all sorts lined the roadside: chariots, chaises, landaus, carts, wagons, whiskies, gigs, phaetons... filled within and surrounded without by faces all glee and delight... The old law of the Forest, that his Majesty must be presented with two milk-white

The Queen's House and the Church at Lyndhurst

greyhounds . . . gathered multitudes together to see the show.' This custom dated back to Norman times, and went with the ownership of the Manor of Bury; George III is thought to have been the last monarch to receive the greyhounds. Fanny Burney described the house as 'Quite unimproved and unrepaired' from the time of Charles II, but she loved Lyndhurst and its loyal people. 'On the Sunday we all went to the parish church; and after the service, instead of a psalm, imagine our surprise to hear the whole congregation join in "God save the King". Misplaced as this was in a church, its intent was so kind, loyal and affectionate, that I believe there was not a dry eye amongst either singers or hearers.'

In Norman times there were four courts of justice to administer the laws of the New Forest. One of these survives in altered form, officially known as the 'Court of Swainmote and Attachment', but generally called the Verderers' Court, where Forest affairs are still settled. The Forest has its own officers, such as verderers, rangers and agistors, with varying duties. Forest commoners have the right to attend the Verderers' Court. The Verderers' Hall, or Court House, was first built, near the Manor House, in 1388, but as it stands now it is mainly Tudor, with later additions. It has fine Tudor chimney-stacks, and contains some interesting old furniture together with various relics of the Forest's history. The Deputy Surveyor of the

New Forest, local representative of the Forestry Commission, also had his office in this building.

Close to the Queen's House, on a mound, stands the church, St. Michael and All Angels, built about 1860 in the typical Gothic Revival style of that date. The charming little Georgian church which Fanny Burney and the Royal party attended was unfortunately pulled down in 1859. The present church is a wonderful example of the period and includes windows by Burne-Jones, William Morris and Kemp, also a very fine fresco behind the altar, of the parable of the wise and foolish virgins, by Lord Leighton, carved wooden angels in the roof, and many other fascinating features. In the churchyard is the grave of Mrs. Hargreaves, the original 'Alice' of *Alice in Wonderland*. She lived in the parish, but her house no longer stands.

Just outside Lyndhurst, on the Brockenhurst road, is Foxlease, the Girl Guides' Training Centre, given to the Movement by Mrs. Archbold in 1922. Princess Mary, President of the Girl Guides' Association, gave a large sum of money, from her wedding presents, to help put the house in order, and Guides and friends from all over the world helped to furnish it. The house stands on the site of a Forest Keeper's Lodge. The north wing is early Georgian, and inside are some rooms with beautiful plaster ceilings, 'Gothic' walls, cornices and fireplaces in the Adam style, believed to be in imitation of Horace Walpole's Strawberry Hill. In 1912 a large, red-tiled and timbered south wing was added. The garden and park are beautiful, and camping and all sorts of other Guide activities take place there, as well as in the Forest round about. Foxlease may be visited by those really interested, by permission of the Guider in charge.

Three miles along the A35 from Lyndhurst to Bournemouth is a cross-roads, sign-posted 'Rhinefield' on the left, with roads leading into the Forest across cattle grids. A little way along the right-hand road, in a clearing on the right, is the Knightwood Oak, supposed to be one of the oldest, and certainly one of the biggest, oaks in the Forest. The road leads on to Mark Ash, where some of the loveliest beeches can be found. Many have tall, straight, majestic trunks, and others have fascinating gnarled, twisted trunks and roots in which pixies, whose existence in the Forest was believed in until quite recently, might be expected to lurk. The pale green foliage of the beeches in the early summer, and the golden, rust and flame colours in the autumn, are of a most indescribable beauty.

Beyond the beech wood is the Bolderwood Arboretum of exotic trees, mainly conifers, planted about 100 years ago. On the opposite side of the A35 is Rhinefield Drive, a charming way through to Brockenhurst. The Drive is lined with rhododendrons, and there is

New Forest beeches

another arboretum, including giant redwoods and other tall conifers, some reaching almost 150 feet. There are pretty little streams, too, in this part of the Forest, and some delightful walks.

Certain areas of the Forest are reserved as car parks and camping grounds, but, through the greater part of it, walkers and horse riders can pursue their way undisturbed by modern contrivances. Brockenhurst is mainly a residential railway junction on the main Waterloo–Bournemouth line. A little way east of the village, south of the railway, is the old church, St. Nicholas, the only church in the New Forest mentioned in the Domesday Book. Standing on a round hill, it has a Norman south door, nave and font. Other parts are of the thirteenth, fourteenth, fifteenth, sixteenth and eighteenth centuries and there is a Royal Arms of Queen Anne. In the north part of the churchyard is the grave of 'Brusher' Mills, a New Forest character of Victorian times, who lived in a wigwam and made his living by catching adders, though it is not quite clear who bought them.

Just off the road from Brockenhurst to Lymington is Boldre, which has a church on a hillside, a little apart from the village. It is partly Norman, partly Early English, and partly Decorated. There is a monument to John Kempe, d. 1652, M.P. for Lymington in the Long Parliament. William Gilpin, author of the well known book *Forest Scenery* and other works which contributed greatly to people's appreciation of the Forest, was Rector there from 1777 until his death in 1804.

Lymington is about five miles south of Brockenhurst. Readers whose first taste of the magic of the New Forest came from reading *The Children of the New Forest* by Captain Marryat will always think of Lymington as the place where Jacob Armitage did his shopping and sold his venison. Captain Marryat did not live actually in the Forest, but had a house at Chewton Glen, now a hotel, between Highcliffe and New Milton. Arnewood is a district near Sway, west of the Brockenhurst–Lymington road. Close to the place where the Beverleys' house is supposed to have stood before being burnt by the Roundheads, now stands Peterson's Tower, a concrete building 218 feet high, with 330 steps. It was built by Judge Peterson, an Indian judge, 1879–85, to relieve local unemployment and to prove that concrete was a good building material. He had a lamp placed at the top of the tower, but Trinity House objected to this on the grounds that it was confusing to sailors, so the tower remains as a daytime landmark for miles around. Peterson's ashes were buried at the foot of the tower, but the people who bought it after his death objected to this, so the ashes were removed to Sway churchyard, and interred in his wife's grave. Jacob Armitage would be astonished at the tower, and surprised, too, to see Lymington as it is now, with the largely Georgian High Street, Yacht Clubs and vast masses of sailing boats where the Boldre, or Lymington, River flows into the Solent, and the large, rather ungainly ferries carrying cars to the Isle of Wight. Lymington is a beautiful and most historic town. The first Charter dates from over 700 years ago, and there was life in the district very much earlier than that. Buckland Rings, a mile north of the town on the Brocken-hurst road, is an earthwork with a fine triple rampart of the Iron Age. Ampress Hole, another earthwork, where the Passford Brook and Lymington River join, is thought to have been a dock of Saxon date.

The town flourished in Norman times under the de Redvers family. Ship-building was one of Lymington's principal industries from medieval times until the eighteenth century. In the fourteenth century Lymington provided twice as many ships for an attack on France as did Portsmouth. It was also an important trading port. Another industry was salt-making, by a process of drying out the salt from the sea water. The salterns lie just south-west of the town, but are no longer used, rock-salt from Cheshire and elsewhere having taken the place of the sea-salt.

In the Civil War, Lymington mainly supported the Parliament. A path across the old salterns leads to Keyhaven, a pretty little harbour for small sailing boats, and nearby is Hurst Castle, where Charles I was imprisoned. This was one of a series of forts erected by Henry VIII all along the south coast from Kent to Cornwall, as a protection against an expected French invasion. The original fort is now much concealed by two heavy Victorian wings, which dwarf it. Charles I was brought there in November 1648 from the Isle of Wight, where

Hurst Castle; from an old print

Lymington

he had been on parole. When told where he was being taken, he remarked, 'You could not have named a worse'. A party of Lymingtonians, including the Mayor, Bernard Knapton, joined in an unsuccessful attempt by Prince Charles to rescue his father. King Charles's stay at Hurst Castle was short. He was soon moved from there to Windsor, and thence to London, for the Trial that ended in his death.

In 1685, Lymington raised a troop of horses for the Duke of Monmouth, whose supporters met at the Knaptons' house, now Monmouth House, now used as a nursing home, a very fine late seventeenth-century house in High Street. In the eighteenth century, Lymington became a fashionable resort and had a small Spa. The Rev. Richard Warner, writing in 1776, describes Lymington as noted for its high moral standards and very beautiful girls. The historian, Edward Gibbon, was M.P. for Lymington for a short time.

Two of the chief families connected with the town were the Powletts and the Burrard Neales. From the top of High Street there is a good view of a monument to Admiral Sir Harry Burrard Neale, similar to Cleopatra's Needle, on a hill across the harbour. In addition to his fame as a sailor, he was also noted in the town for presenting the iron columns for the town's first gas lamps. This is commemorated by a very fine gas lamp on a Doric column, standing on the Quay, 'a tribute of respect and gratitude for his munificent gift'.

The Church of St. Thomas the Apostle near the top of High Street has a partly Early English chancel, a tower built in 1670, with an eighteenth-century cupola, late eighteenth-century galleries, and a Royal Arms of 1676, but with the 'C' of Charles altered to the 'G' of George to save expense. Another interesting building is the Community Centre, a pioneer of its kind, started by Mr. Hole soon after World War II and now copied all over the country. Part of the building is a picturesque old Malt House, and modern additions are in good taste. During the French Revolution, some of the emigrés were lodged there.

The town has, besides boat-building, some modern industries, but they lie on the outskirts and do not interfere in any way with the architectural charm of the High Street and the old streets near the Quay.

CHAPTER III

Beaulieu to Southampton

Five miles to the north-east of Lymington is Beaulieu. The name means 'Beautiful Place' and is pronounced 'Bewley'. It is a charming village situated at the head of a tidal creek of great beauty. In 1204, King John founded a great Cistercian Abbey here, and as time went on, it became a well known Sanctuary resorted to by several distinguished people, among them being Queen Margaret of Anjou, wife of Henry VI, during the Wars of the Roses; the Countess of Warwick, widow of Warwick the King Maker; and the imposter, Perkin Warbeck, during the reign of Henry VII. At the Dissolution the Abbey Church, a magnificent building, was speedily destroyed, and the stones used for building forts along the Solent coast, Hurst Castle and Calshot Castle. The foundations have been dug out, and help to show what a vast building the Abbey Church was. Of the conventional buildings of the monastery, the Cloister Court remains, around which the various buildings were disposed. The church was on the north side, the Chapter House, or meeting place of the monks, on the east, the Refectory on the south, and the lay brothers', or servants, quarters on the west. This last building is still partly preserved intact, and has a most interesting museum on the ground floor, and a restaurant above. Of the Chapter House, only the three great arches which formerly led into it have survived. The Refectory became the village church, and is a beautiful building in the Early English style. It was the custom in most monasteries for the meal to be taken in silence, while one of the brethren ascended into a pulpit and read aloud to the monks. The beautiful pulpit still survives, being approached by steps contained in the thickness of the wall. The blocked hatch leading into the former kitchen, now destroyed, is still to be seen.

The Palace, now occupied by Lord Montagu, was the former gatehouse of the monastery. It has been converted into a spacious residence by blocking up the entrance arches. A short distance northwards from the Abbey is the Motor Museum, established by Lord Montagu in memory of his father, who had been a pioneer motorist. The whole evolution of the motor car may be studied, from the very earliest examples with tiller steering, solid tyres and carriage bodies. It is difficult to believe that these queer 'horseless carriages', as they were called, are the direct ancestors of the modern motor car, for which we allow large stretches of good agricultural land to be converted into wastes of concrete.

Two miles down the Beaulieu River is St. Leonard's, which was a grange or farm belonging to the monks. There was an enormous spicarium or barn, the ruins of which still stand. Inside is another, smaller barn, still in use, and the size of the larger barn can be realised by entering the smaller one. The original barn was 216 feet long and 60 feet high. Adjoining it is a ruined chapel, dating from c. 1300.

Three miles south of Beaulieu is the charming hamlet of Buckler's Hard, consisting mainly of two terraces of old red brick cottages, one now a Chapel, with wide verges running downhill to the river. In the eighteenth century, John, Duke of Montagu, hoped to establish a port here for trade with the sugar-producing islands of St. Lucia and St. Vincent, and to re-name Buckler's Hard 'Montaguville', but the scheme came to nothing. In 1744, the first naval vessel, *Surprise*, was built at Buckler's Hard by Joseph and James Wyatt. In 1749 Henry Adams, a noted ship-builder, was sent to Buckler's Hard by the Navy Board. Under him, many of the 'wooden walls' of England were built. These included the famous warships *Agamemnon*, *Illustrious*, *Swiftsure* and *Euryalus*, all of which fought at Trafalgar. When each ship reached a certain stage of building, it was towed

A 19th Century view of the ruins of Beaulieu Abbey

across to Portsmouth by sailors in rowing boats, for completion. After about 1800 the dockyard was closed and Buckler's Hard, instead of being a hive of industry, was silent and deserted for a time. However, during World War II, naval motor launches for anti-submarine and air-sea rescue work were built there. Parts of the 'Mulberry Harbour' scheme used in the Normandy landings were also built nearby. In 1963, a most interesting Maritime Museum was established by Lord Montagu of Beaulieu, and opened by Admiral of the Fleet Lord Mountbatten of Burma. The 'Master Builders' House', Henry Adams' home, near the old Hard, has become a popular hotel, and in the summer there are frequent boat trips down the river.

Buckler's Hard has now become a popular resort, but only a few miles away modern industry flourishes on a vast scale. Eastward from Beaulieu, in complete contrast, across an extensive heath lies the huge Fawley Oil Refinery on the western shore of Southampton Water. Enormous tankers come alongside to discharge their cargo.

Hampshire lost many churches during World War II, and among them were those of Fawley and Dibden, both near the shores of Southampton Water. Lying in ruins for some years after the end of the war, they were finally rebuilt and much beautified. At the head of Southampton Water, where the Test flows into it, is Eling, a village which retains its rural charm in spite of the neighbourhood of the sprawling Southampton suburb, Totton. Isaac Watts, the well-known eighteenth-century divine and hymnologist, was inspired by the view from Eling churchyard to write the favourite hymn, 'There is a land of pure delight'. Across the Test from where he sat were the 'sweet fields beyond the swelling floods', where today can be seen only the vast spread of Southampton and its suburbs, with industries, housing estates and skyscraper blocks of flats.

The city and port of Southampton owe their origin to the establishment of a Roman station at Clausentum, now Bitterne, which lies in a loop of the Itchen on the eastern shore. This in due course gave place to a Saxon settlement at a point then known as Hamweh, which was situated on the opposite shore of the Itchen. When the Normans came, they placed their town on the promontory between the rivers Itchen and Test. Across the neck of the peninsula they dug a ditch and rampart, and placed in the middle of it a Norman gateway. This original gateway still exists at the Bargate, though much added to in later centuries. Additions during the fourteenth and fifteenth centuries have made it one of the most imposing gateways in the country.

The coming of electric trams during the early years of the twentieth century nearly caused the downfall of the Bargate. The town was completely divided on the subject and feelings ran high. Finally it

Southampton Bargate from the north, in the 19th century

was settled by lowering the roadway to allow a tram to pass through. One had to sit tight or be electrocuted when sitting on the top of the tram! Later the upper decks of the trams were closed in and only a few feet clearance allowed, and this solved the problem, but young people of those days sadly missed the the thrill of 'shooting the Bargate'.

In the late thirteenth and early fourteenth centuries, walls were constructed along the north and east sides of the town and, in view of the proximity of the Test on the west side, were considered sufficient defence. Unfortunately, this was disproved, for the French successfully invaded Southampton in 1338, murdering, looting and destroying almost the entire town. This disastrous happening caused the citizens to complete the circuit of the walls along the western shore where, at high tide, the water lapped the walls. All this part has since been reclaimed.

Along the Western Shore were houses. The wall here was carried on arches known as the Arcades, and was built into the fronts of the original houses standing there. One of them is a Norman house, a domestic dwelling of the twelfth century. A Norman chimney from another house, revealed by the bombardment in World War II, has been re-erected here. In the blocking of a Norman window is a gun-port dating from c. 1360, a very early example.

Southampton Bargate today from the south

At the north end of the old town was the Castle, a strong fortress of Norman times. It was a Royal Castle, and many monarchs stayed there, the last being Queen Elizabeth I. When she visited the town in 1591, she was received at the Bargate and given a tremendous welcome. She graciously accepted a purse of £40. In 1669, Charles II also received a purse at the Bargate, on this occasion amounting to 150 guineas. During the early nineteenth century, the Marquess of Lansdowne erected a pseudo-Gothic castle on the mound, which only lasted for a few years and, after its demolition, the mound was lowered. A tall block of flats now stands upon it. At the south-east corner of the old town is a 'spur-work', jutting out into what was once water, but is now reclaimed land. This is God's House Tower, called after a neighbouring almshouse, founded in 1197, but rebuilt in Victorian times. Now a most interesting Museum of Archaeology, it was formerly used as a gaol. Before that, in the fifteenth century, it was the headquarters of the Town Gunner, a most important individual, who received a salary of 6d. a day. Compared with this, the salary of 1s. a week paid, in 1563, to six men and women for nursing victims of the plague seems rather meagre, since their task must have been quite as dangerous as, and more disagreeable than, that of the gunner. In 1457 the French attempted a landing, but when the Tower guns came into action they promptly retreated.

Opposite the Royal Pier is the old wool warehouse, dating from the fourteenth century. West country wool was stored there before

Victorian engraving of the walls of Southampton

being exported to Flanders, one of the great cloth-making countries. During the Napoleonic wars, French prisoners were confined in the woolhouse, and some carved their names on the roof timbers. The building is now a fascinating Maritime Museum.

A short distance westward are two memorials of great historic interest. One is to the memory of the Pilgrim Fathers who, in 1620, sailed from this Quay on their epic voyage to the New World. The other monument, closely adjoining it, is to the memory of a stewardess who gave up her lifebelt to a passenger, when the *Stella* went on the rocks at the Casquets in the Channel Islands in 1899. Beyond this again is the West Gate. It echoed to the tramp of armed men on two historic occasions; in 1346 when the troops embarked for France, for the campaign which led to the great victory of Crécy, and again in 1415 before the Agincourt campaign. The Westgate leads to St. Michael's Church, which was originally Norman, but has been much rebuilt. The church contains a magnificent Tournai marble font, of which there are only seven in England, and many other points of interest.

Opposite the church is the Tudor House, where Henry VIII and Anne Boleyn once stayed. This is a very good example of a Tudor merchant's house. It is one of Southampton's four museums, and contains some fascinating period rooms. Close by is High Street which has been entirely rebuilt since World War II, when most of it was flattened by bombs. Curiously enough, neither the Bargate nor any other old building, except the Church of the Holy Rood, was harmed, though so near to other buildings which were destroyed. Holy Rood lost its spire and was completely burnt out. The ruins of this church have been made safe and a garden laid out, commemorating the men of the Merchant Navy who were killed in the course of their duties.

A few doors further north is the Dolphin Hotel, a very handsome Georgian building dating from the time when Southampton had gained fame as a Spa, to which people of rank and fashion resorted after the discovery of a chalybeate spring. Spas were very much in vogue in the eighteenth century, and wherever there was a spring of water with even the mildest medicinal qualities the owner would try to develop a Spa. Southampton had the additional advantage of sea bathing. There was a good bathing beach on the western shore, where the New Docks are now, and Frederick, Prince of Wales, bathed there in 1750, and so started the fashion. The spring was north of the Bargate and gardens, a Reading Room and other amenities were set up around it. A basin for the spring water, with a fluted pedestal, can be seen in the Tudor House Museum. The water was supposed to cure jaundice, scurvy, and all sorts of complaints, and the sea bathing was good for rheumatism, and was believed to cure, among other things, the bites of mad dogs. The Long Room, or Assembly Room, to be found in any important Spa, was built near the Westgate, and was under a Master of the Ceremonies, whose rule was law. As part of the rules, swords had to be left at the door; gentlemen could not dance in boots, nor ladies in aprons, mittens or black gloves; dances had to begin at seven o'clock and end punctually at eleven o'clock, even in the middle of a dance; and cards must not be played on Sundays. Jane Austen and her mother lived in Southampton from 1806 to 1809, and Jane probably attended balls, routs and card-parties of a genteel description, sometimes at the Dolphin Hotel, which had a beautiful Assembly Room, now a dining room, with very large bow-windows. Jane gave amusing accounts of the life in her letters to her sister Cassandra. 'Commerce' seems to have been the favourite card game, and there were musical parties, pleasant walks, and boating on the Itchen.

The Star Inn, near the Dolphin, was another Hotel which became important during the Spa period, and there were several other good inns, and many handsome dwellings built to house the people who flocked to Southampton. When, however, the Prince Regent, later George IV, frequently visited Brighton instead of Southampton, the world of fashion went with him, and Southampton became neglected, and the Spa disused. With the coming of the railway, the town became industrialised and the docks were built, and Southampton became one of the chief ports of the world.

At the north end of the High Street, here called 'Above Bar', are two memorials, one a cenotaph commemorating the dead of both world wars, and the other to those who perished when the *Titanic* went down on her maiden voyage in 1912. A less serious memorial is the Canute public house, in Canute Road, near the docks. According to legend this is where Canute sat on his throne on the seashore, and proved to his foolishly flattering courtiers that even he could not control the tides.

Several well known people were born in Southampton, one being Isaac Watts whose most famous hymn, 'O God, our Help in Ages past' is now played upon the carillon at the Civic Centre. There is also a statue of Watts in the pleasant open space in the middle of the town known as the Marlands. The name is a corruption of 'Mary Magdalen', because a Leper Hospital, dedicated to her, once stood in the vicinity. Other natives were Charles Dibdin, 1745–1814, composer of many nautical ballads including 'Tom Bowling', and Sir John Millais, the famous Victorian artist, 1829–97.

Southampton Docks, with the old 'Queen Mary' seen at the Ocean Terminal

No visitor to Southampton should miss seeing Netley Abbey, reached by ferry to Woolston. The ruins are set in beautiful sylvan surroundings, and one can understand Horace Walpole saying in 1755, 'They are not the ruins of Netley, but of Paradise. Oh! the purple Abbots, what a spot had they chosen to slumber in!' Since then, innumerable poets have sung the praises of this beautiful ruin. Netley Abbey was to have been founded by Peter des Roches, Bishop of Winchester, but his death prevented this. However, the Abbey was colonised by Cistercian monks from Beaulieu in 1239. Henry III, moved to pity by the new monastery and its poverty, decided to become its founder and patron. On the base of one of the great pillars formerly supporting the central tower is a dedicatory inscription, 'H.DI. GRA REX ANGL.' The plan of the monastic buildings very much resembled that of the mother house of Beaulieu. In spite of its being a Royal Foundation, Netley was still a poor house when it was dissolved. The site and buildings were then granted to Sir William Paulet, later Marquess of Winchester, who converted the Abbey Church and the east range of the cloister court into a large mansion. It is a curious fact that, although there are very few remains of this mansion, the ruins of the monastery survive to a considerable extent. They are mostly in the very beautiful Early English style of the mid-thirteenth century, but much was lost at the Dissolution. Paulet demolished the arcades of the nave, which he converted into his hall and kitchen. Except for a Tudor doorway leading into the Cloister Court, nothing remains of these buildings. Paulet's alterations may be readily distinguished from the medieval work, as they are in red brick.

The Abbey is entered through a Tudor gatehouse built on the site of the Refectory, which was demolished. This gateway gave entrance to the Cloister Court, which became Paulet's garden. In the middle of the Court he erected a fountain, of which the base remains.

The east portion of the church dates from the thirteenth century, but the nave was not finished until the fourteenth century, c. 1290–1320. The great west window has lost its tracery, but that in the east window survives. In 1770 the north transept was taken down and re-erected as a sham ruin in Cranbury Park, Otterbourne, when it was fashionable to have either a tower or a sham ruin in one's park. The south transept still stands to its full height, and the chapels retain their vaulting. The east range was converted into the main residential portion by Paulet, when the Chapter House and the dormitory above it became private apartments.

Immediately to the south of the south transept is the vestry and sacristy, still retaining their vault; south again is the Chapter House, and south of this the monks' parlour. Still further south is the sub-vault of the dormitory, a long room with a row of columns down the centre, which may have been the novices' day-room; a Tudor fireplace has been inserted into it. At the south-east end of the east range is a vaulted room containing a noble fireplace. This was probably the Infirmary, and adjoining it on the west is a room, probably a kitchen where special food was cooked for sick monks. A serving hatch in the wall indicates where the food was passed through. Above the vaulted room was the rere-dorter, or privies with chutes communicating directly into a stream. A small detached thirteenth-century building to the east of the ruins is thought to have been the Abbot's Lodging. The ground floor is vaulted; on the upper floor was a Chapel, and at the north-east corner a garde-robe.

Early in the eighteenth century the ruins were sold to Mr. Walter Taylor, a Southampton builder. When he was superintending the destruction of the great west window, the stones of it fell on him, causing his instant death. After this, no one would have anything more to do with demolition, as it was believed that the wrath of God would cause a curse to light upon anyone who attempted it. After the ruins had been used for many years as a place for the holding of 'beanfeasts' accompanied by music and dancing, they were placed in the guardianship of the Ministry of Works, now the Department of the Environment. Though Netley had been robbed and ill-treated for many years, it has been beautifully restored, and forms one of the loveliest of all the monastic ruins in the country.

A very good plan is on exhibition, and an excellent guide book is available.

CHAPTER IV

The Test Valley

About ten miles up the Test Valley from Southampton lies Romsey, with its magnificent Abbey Church. A Nunnery was founded there in the early tenth century, probably by Edward the Elder, son of Alfred the Great, and Edward's daughter Elfleda was the first Abbess. Many other royal ladies took the veil at this Nunnery, and several were Abbesses. The Abbey was reconstituted in 967 by Edgar, grandson of Edward, as a Benedictine Nunnery. Two beautiful, carved Saxon crucifixes remain from these early times. One, found facing inwards into a wall, probably to protect it from sixteenth century reformers, is now a reredos in one of the east chapels. The other, life-size, and with the hand of God above the figure of Christ, is outside the south door of the nave, known as the Abbess's door, in what was formerly the cloister court. This is probably early eleventh century.

In 1160 King Stephen's daughter, Mary, became Abbess, and his brother, Henri de Blois, Bishop of Winchester, rebuilt the greater part of the church in the splendid Norman style in which it still stands. The foundations of the apse of the Saxon Church, which had been replaced by the Norman one, were discovered by chance in 1900, during the course of some repairs. The Norman work was carried on as far as the third bay of the nave, but there the work was discontinued, and when it was resumed some time later, it was in the Early English style, with beautiful capitals. The junction of the Norman and Early English work in the triforium arches is very striking. In the north chancel aisle there is a Norman capital carved with a very spirited battle scene, with various pieces of the combatants lying on the ground, while angels are trying to stop the fighting by taking hold of the swords.

Among many other beautiful and interesting features of the Abbey is a sixteenth century wooden reredos, in the north transept; the paintings include the Resurrection, with angels and soldiers, and a row of saints above. A scene of Christ in Glory was unfortunately lost in 1829. In this transept is also a memorial window to the Rev. E. L. Berthon, inventor of a collapsible boat for saving life at sea.

The Larger Saxon Rood at Romsey Abbey
(First half of 11th century)

The Norman south transept of Romsey Abbey

Monuments include one to John St. Barbe Baker with his wife and children, 1658, believed to be by Thomas Stanton, master of the Mason's Company, one of a family of sculptors, and a beautiful memorial statue by Fuchs to Maud Ashley with one of her daughters, 1911. She was the mother of Lady Mountbatten, who was greatly beloved in Romsey and did much for the town, as well as for the Save the Children Fund and other good causes. There is a thirteenth-century, Purbeck marble effigy of a lady in the south transept.

The north wall of the exterior of the Abbey has some bullet scars from the Civil War, and there is a quaint 'fertility figure' rather like those at Sopley.

The Nunnery had not always been noted for its high moral tone; at various times it had 'visitations' and the nuns had been found to be leading very lax lives and to be frequenting taverns. Just before the Dissolution, however, they had an inspection and everything was found in good order, and Henry VIII confirmed their various Royal Charters. It must have been a very severe shock to them, therefore, when, only about a year later, he commanded the Nunnery to be dissolved and all the buildings demolished. The townspeople, who had previously used just the north aisle of the Abbey Church as their Parish Church, were allowed to purchase the whole building for £100, and the Deed of Sale, signed by Henry VIII, is still preserved.

East of the Abbey, in a yard across Church Street, is King John's Hunting Lodge, built by him in the thirteenth century, and discovered by chance amid some slum property by W. J. Andrew, F.S.A., in 1927. At one time a guest house of the Abbess, it became, after the Dissolution, a private residence, and later a workhouse. It has windows with dog-tooth ornaments, and inside, on the plaster walls, a set of coats of arms was scratched by some Barons who stayed there in 1306.

Although the town is so old, its first Charter of Incorporation as a Borough dates only from the time of James I. At one time Romsey was a wool town, as is shown by the 'Bishop Blaise' Inn, he being the patron saint of wool-combers. Brewing has been another of the chief industries of the town. There are other interesting inns. The White Horse in the Market Place dates from Tudor times but has a Georgian front. It still has much of the old timber-work, and there are wall-paintings in the bar and lounge. On the first floor of the Tudor Rose there is a sixteenth-century timber-framed room with a stone fireplace, and the Dolphin has pleasant bow-windows. A more sinister feature is the iron bracket from which hung the sign of the former Swan, also in the Market Place. A soldier, who had committed a murder during the Civil War, was hanged from this bracket.

In the Market Place is a statue of Lord Palmerston, who was born and lived at Broadlands, a fine house of white brick designed by Henry Holland in 1760, standing on the bank of the Test just west of the town. It is now the seat of Lord Mountbatten of Burma, and Queen Elizabeth II, as Princess Elizabeth, spent part of her honeymoon there. Palmerston was one of the most colourful and controversial political figures of Victorian times, both as Foreign Minister and Prime Minister. Handsome, gallant and gay, warm-hearted, sometimes irritable and tactless, always full of self-confidence, he was adored by many people and detested by others. Queen Victoria and Prince Albert disapproved of him strongly, not only because his private life was not up to their very high standards, but also because they thought that his foreign policy was anti-German. In fact, it was not directed particularly against any country, but was devoted to preserving peace through the Balance of Power, and Palmerston supported any country whose strength, he felt, would best serve this end. A powerful Britain, he believed, would be valuable and useful to the whole world, and any British subject was entitled, in his view, to the support of the British Navy. He was in favour of moderate Parliamentary Reform, and against slavery and any form of tyranny or despotism.

In his young days, when he was Minister of War, he came under the lash of Cobbett's pen, because a poacher on the Broadlands estate was hanged for shooting at, and seriously injuring, one of the gamekeepers.

Statue of Palmerston, Romsey

Cobbett, the author of *Rural Rides*, was always ready to find fault
with the aristocracy, and he sometimes had grounds for his complaints, as the differences between rich and poor were far too great at
that time, but in this case he was unjust to Palmerston, who was much
distressed about this verdict and did his best, though unsuccessfully,
to have the poacher reprieved. Cobbett was sympathetic towards
poachers, because they badly needed the game which they poached,
but the Judge at the Hampshire Assizes considered that no game-
keeper's life would be safe if this man was not hanged, so the law
took its course, to Palmerston's sorrow.

In spite of his preoccupation with affairs of state, Palmerston always
found time to take an interest in the people and affairs of Romsey.
'We had a tea-party for the children of the Romsey School, to
celebrate Miss Oliphant's successful exertion as school-mistress for
fifty years', he wrote to a friend. It is pleasant to think of him enjoy-
ing himself with the children, and remarkable to think that there
had been a school in Romsey for fifty years, when schools were by
no means common. Education was not made compulsory until 1876,
and was not free until 1891, years after Palmerston's death.

Another of his Hampshire interests was a scheme for the drainage
of the Test Valley from Whitchurch to Redbridge, and a less local
one was a plan for the improvement of the sanitation of London,
which was in such a shocking state that it killed hundreds of people
every year. One very wrong thing that he did was to encourage, or at
least to fail completely to discourage, the opium trade in China, but
he must have had a little idea of the evils which would result from it.
He had a series of forts built on Portsdown, in case of a possible
French invasion.

He had entered Parliament at the age of twenty-three, as member
for the 'rotten borough' of Newtown, Isle of Wight, where hardly
anyone lived, on the curious condition that he would never, even at
an election, set foot in the place. In 1855, at the age of seventy, he
became Prime Minister, and steered the country to victory in the
Crimean War. He was at the height of his popularity at this time.
With one short break as Leader of the Opposition, he remained Prime
Minister until his death, in office, at the age of eighty-one.

A frequent visitor to Broadlands in Palmerston's time was the young
Florence Nightingale, whose family lived at Embley Park, now a boys'
school, west of Romsey. She was a beautiful and charming girl, who
could have been a great social success and made a very suitable marriage to Richard Monckton Milnes. She was, indeed, torn between her
love for him and her feeling that she was being definitely called by
God to take up nursing. Her mother and sister did their best to push

Lord Palmerston

her into the marriage, and there were hysterical scenes at Embley, but eventually Florence's sense of vocation prevailed and, with tremendous courage and perseverance, she embarked on a nursing career. She trained first at Kaiserwerth on the Rhine, and later at the Hospital for Sick Gentlewomen in Harley Street.

She had to overcome mountains of prejudice before, helped by Sidney Herbert, Secretary for War, she was allowed to take a party of nurses out to the Crimean War in 1854. Her work there, in the conditions of almost indescribable filth in the hospitals, and her reduction of the death rate among the wounded from 42 per cent to about 2 per cent, is too well known to need re-telling. She was a hard task-mistress, and spared neither herself nor the nurses who worked under her, but probably she could not have managed all that she did if she had allowed herself to be too soft or sympathetic with her staff. The patients adored her, and so did many of the nurses in spite of her severity. After the war, her health having suffered considerably, she devoted herself mainly to organising work. She founded the Nightingale Training Schools for nurses at St. Thomas's and King's College Hospitals, London, chose the site of the present Winchester Hospital, and continued the good work of improving conditions of nursing in the army. She raised the whole profession of nursing, in which the majority of nurses had previously been dirty and drunken 'Sarah Gamps', to the honoured position which it holds today. Although she was a semi-invalid, she lived to the age of ninety. She received the Order of Merit from Edward VII in 1907, but was hardly able to appreciate it. She died in 1910, and was buried quietly in Wellow churchyard, near her old home.

Besides Florence Nightingale's grave, and a tablet to her memory, East Wellow Church has the remains of some very interesting wall-paintings, a painted design of lilies and roses on the thirteenth-century walls of the nave and chancel, a fine timbered roof of the same century, and an east window, believed to date from 1220, with the heads of two kings above it, possibly John and Henry III. There are also Jacobean stalls, altar-rail and panelling in the chancel, and timber posts dividing the nave from the sixteenth-century south aisle.

Michelmersh, a little way up the Test valley to the east, has a church with a wooden tower, of which there are two or three in Hampshire.

Mottisfont, about three miles from Romsey and west of the Test, was another Hampshire Abbey, founded as an Augustinian Priory c. 1200. Like Netley, it was converted at the Dissolution into a Tudor private house, by William, Lord Sandys. He retained the thirteenth-century undercroft of the west range of the conventual buildings, parts

Florence Nightingale

Michelmersh church

of the chapter house and some other portions of the Abbey, which are curiously incorporated into the house. The mansion was extended, and the south side rebuilt, in the eighteenth century. In the present drawing-room is a wonderful example of 'trompe l'oeil' mural painting, carried out in 1938–9 by Rex Whistler, the brilliant young artist, who was killed in the Normandy landings in 1944. It is so effective that the room really seems like a Gothic Hall belonging to the old Abbey. There are good Georgian-style stables, with a cupola and two wings, dating from 1837. The gardens, with beautiful trees, run down to the Test. Mottisfont Abbey is National Trust property, and is open from April to September on Wednesdays and Thursdays, 2.15–5.30 p.m.

St. Andrew's Church at Mottisfont has a Norman nave and chancel arch, a Perpendicular chancel, a fine fifteenth-century stained glass east window, a beautiful head of Christ in the north-west window of the chancel, *c.* 1320, and the badge of Edward IV in the north-east window. The pulpit and altar are of seventeenth century work.

Stockbridge, further up the Test, is a little town, once notorious as the most corrupt of all the 'rotten boroughs'. It was said that each vote cost the candidate £60. The Test about here is noted for its trout fishing. The town consists mainly of one wide street, with many charming houses, including an old coaching inn, the Grosvenor Hotel,

The River Test near Mottisfont

with a projecting porch. Branches of the Test run through bridges under the street in several places. The church in the middle of the town dates from 1863, but includes a Norman font, some windows and other relics of the old Church of St. Peter, at the east end of the town. In this old church, of which only the chancel now remains, Robert, Earl of Gloucester took sanctuary in 1141, after fighting to cover the retreat of the Empress Matilda, who was being pursued from Winchester by Stephen's soldiers. Thanks to Gloucester's action, Matilda escaped, but he himself was taken prisoner.

At the other end of the town, in Houghton Road, is a house where Welsh cattle-drovers used to stay when driving cattle from Wales to London. It still has a Welsh inscription, meaning 'Good Accommodation'.

North-west of Stockbridge is Danebury Hill, a magnificent Iron Age stronghold, which has been, and is still being excavated, under the direction of Professor Barry Cunliffe, F.S.A. The entrance has three lines of ramparts and ditches, enclosing an area of 13 acres. The lines of defences are, in places, 16 feet high and 60 feet broad. On the east side is a labyrinthine entrance with extremely strong defences, from which assailants could be taken in the flank. This is the finest Iron Age stronghold in Hampshire, comparable with the famous fortress of Maiden Castle in Dorset.

South and west of Danebury are the amusingly named Nether

Stockbridge

Wallop, Middle Wallop and Over Wallop, very pretty villages on the Wallop brook. Nether Wallop has a good Transition-Norman Church, with wall-paintings, including St. George and the Dragon, and a fine brass in the nave floor to Mary Gore, 1436, Prioress of Amesbury Nunnery, Wiltshire. This is the only known brass of a Prioress in England. The Norman north doorway is the oldest work in the church.

Andover, north-east of the Wallops, is now largely a vast new industrial town, but its centre is a pleasant old market town with some charming inns, including the Angel in High Street, parts of which are fifteenth century, and the very handsome Star and Garter in the Market Place, with a bow-windowed Regency front. Traditionally, Andover is the site of Ethelred the Unready's first payment of 'Danegeld' to Olaf the Dane. Six mills were mentioned in Andover in the Domesday survey, and a very pretty one, the Old Town Mill, still exists in Western Avenue and is being made into a Youth Centre. The town's first Charter of Incorporation was granted in 1100 by King John, who is said to have stayed at the Angel, which already existed as an inn, though it was later completely destroyed by fire. In medieval times, Andover was a flourishing wool town and, like Romsey and other towns, it has a 'Bishop Blaise' Inn as witness to this fact.

During the Civil War, Charles I had a successful skirmish with the

Roundheads, and afterwards stayed the night at the Star and Garter. On the whole, however, the town was Parliamentarian in its sympathies, and the Vicar, who was a Royalist, was driven out and is said to have escaped over the roofs of East Street, taking with him the church plate. James II, on his way to meet his enemy William of Orange, stayed a night at Andover, probably at the Angel, though some historians say at a private house. While he was there, however, he was persuaded by his advisers that his cause was hopeless, and he decided to abdicate, and to abandon the throne to William and Mary.

In coaching days, Andover was important, being on several main routes, including that from London to Salisbury and the west. St. Mary's Church, standing very well at the top of a rise, is an excellent example of the Gothic Revival, in the thirteenth-century style, though actually built c. 1846. The old church, which formerly stood on the site, was condemned by an architect as unsafe although, in fact, gunpowder had to be used to demolish it. A beautiful Norman doorway from the old church has been used as a gateway from the churchyard to High Street. The churchyard is supposed to be haunted by a strange ghost, of whom all that is seen is one leg in a black stocking!

As early as 1916, the Royal Air Force set up an establishment in Andover and the Freedom of the Borough was given to the R.A.F. in 1955, to mark this long connection. About two miles north of

Wherwell

Andover is Enham Alamein, a village designed for the rehabilitation of disabled soldiers of both world wars.

About three miles south east of Andover's vast urban spread is one of Hampshire's most beautiful villages, Wherwell, in a very pretty part of the Test Valley. It has many charming thatched and timbered cottages. A house called the Priory stands on the site of yet another of Hampshire's Abbeys. This was founded for the Benedictine nuns, c. 986, by Elfrida, widow of King Edgar. She had murdered, or caused to be murdered, her first husband, Ethelwolf, and her stepson Edward the Martyr, and she built Wherwell Abbey to atone for her sins, spending the last part of her life in penitence there. Euphemia, who was Abbess for about thirty years in the thirteenth century, was a very saintly and also a very practical woman, who saw to the maintenance and improvement of the buildings as well as to her nuns' spiritual welfare. At the Dissolution, Wherwell shared the fate of most of the other Abbeys, and Henry VIII granted the property to Thomas West, Lord de la Warr.

The present Church of St. Peter dates from 1856–8, but in it are some fragments from the old church and the Nunnery, including an early Saxon cross-shaft with inter-lacing pattern, two fourteenth-century sculptures, one of the Harrowing of Hell and the other of Christ with Mary Magdalene in the garden, and a fifteenth-century

Whitchurch, Town Hall and White Hart

Whitchurch Mill

effigy of a nun. A steep wooded hill in the background adds to the charm of the village.

Longparish is another very pretty village in the Test Valley, with St. Nicholas Church which is partly thirteenth century with a good Perpendicular tower, but otherwise much restored in the middle of the nineteenth century. There is a William Morris east window.

Farther up the Test Valley is Whitchurch, a pleasant little town with a Georgian town hall with a cupola, and a picturesque coaching inn, the White Hart. This inn had a room called 'the Commandments Room', and for a long time nobody knew why, but, during some alterations, an oil painting of about 1612 was discovered, hidden in a wall, depicting the ten commandments and the punishments for breaking them. It was presumably hidden for safety during the Commonwealth, but was moved into the church after being found in the inn. The Church of All Hallows was very much restored, c. 1866, but has a thirteenth-century south arcade, and a fifteenth-century font, and a very remarkable gravestone, believed to be ninth century, of Frithburga, an Anglo-Saxon lady. It has an inscription in Roman letters, and, in an arched recess in the front, a relief bust of Christ. In Winchester Road there is a silk mill, dating from 1815.

A mile or so east of Whitchurch is Laverstoke, where the paper money is made. Cobbett, the famous nineteenth-century Radical already mentioned, hated the paper money, and attributed to it most of the ills of low wages and general economic distress. 'I hope', he wrote in *Rural Rides* after passing the mill, 'the time will come when a monument will be erected where that mill now stands, and on that monument will be inscribed THE CURSE OF ENGLAND.' On another occasion he wrote, 'O, accursed paper money! Has hell a torment surpassing the wickedness of thy inventors?' He called the makers 'the rag-merchants', and railed on them in season and out. True, agricultural wages were as low as 6s. a week in Hampshire at that time but, as we still have the paper money, and wages are higher here than at any previous time, it seems that the paper must have been a very minor cause of the distress.

CHAPTER V

North-east Hampshire

The country east of Whitchurch is gently sloping Downland, and is mainly agricultural. About half-way between Whitchurch and Basingstoke, and a mile or so south of the B3400 road, is Steventon, where Jane Austen was born and brought up, her father being Rector there for forty years. She lived there from 1770 until 1800, and there wrote *Northanger Abbey* and *Pride and Prejudice*, though they were not published until much later. Unfortunately the old Rectory was demolished, and even a pump, which drew water from the Rectory well and marked the site of the house, was stolen by hooligans.

The Church of St. Nicholas dates from the early thirteenth century. It contains the faint remains of a wall painting, and a Saxon cross-shaft, probably late ninth century, with a pattern of intertwined dragons. There are tombs of Anne Austen, d. 1795, and the Rev. James Austen, d. 1819.

Steventon Manor was the home of the Digweeds in Jane Austen's time, and was no doubt the scene of the sort of party that she describes so well. It had one Tudor wing, and the rest was added in 1875–6 in the Tudor style, but it has unfortunately been left derelict.

In Jane Austen's time, Basingstoke was a quiet little country town where she occasionally did her shopping. It seems to have been inhabited before Roman times, and in Saxon times it was a Royal Manor. A well known native of Basingstoke was Walter de Merton, who founded Merton College Oxford, and was at one time Bishop of Rochester. He built St. John the Baptist Hospital in about 1235, but none of the old buildings now remain. Another benefactor was Sir James Deane, who founded Almshouses in London Street in 1607; these can still be seen. In medieval times Basingstoke had a cloth industry. The first surviving Charter of Incorporation as a Borough was granted by James I in 1623, though there were earlier Charters.

The opening of the Basingstoke Canal in 1789 caused some growth in population and industry, and the coming of the railway in 1839 did more so. Basingstoke was the junction of the Great Western broad gauge and the London and South Western narrow gauge, and Queen

Ancient and modern Basingstoke

Victoria had to change there on her journeys from Windsor to Osborne. In spite of these developments, Basingstoke remained a comparatively small town until the present century. Indeed, Mad Margaret in Gilbert and Sullivan's *Ruddigore* suggested the word 'Basingstoke' as a mental sedative. She could hardly use it in that way now, as Basingstoke is one of the most active and growing towns in Hampshire. After World War I, it had a population of about 14,000: since World War II, it has increased to nearly 60,000, and is expected to rise to 80,000 within the next few years. All round the outskirts of the town are modern industries and housing estates, and at the Town Centre is a very well designed, traffic-free shopping area, with a multi-storey car park above it. From the shopping centre, however, one can step down by a flight of steps or a sloping path, and find oneself back in the old town.

St. Michael's Church, in Church Street, is mainly of early Perpendicular date. The north chapel is a 1914–18 War Memorial, designed by Sir Charles Nicholson. In it is a triptych, thought to have been painted by a pupil of Leonardo da Vinci. The church also contains an Elizabethan alms-box, 1576, and Royal Arms of Elizabeth I, William III and James I. Old glass in the east window was unhappily destroyed by bombing in 1940, and some bomb-marks remain on the outer south wall of the church, but the inside was

Chapel of the Holy Ghost, Basingstoke, in the 19th Century

unharmed. Church Cottage, west of the church, is probably sixteenth century and is listed for preservation.

North of the railway line, in a cemetery, are the remains of two old Chapels, the Chapel of the Holy Ghost, a mortuary chapel of the thirteenth century, and the Holy Trinity Chapel, a chantry added to the other by Bishop Fox and Lord Sandys of the Vyne, in early Tudor times. The cemetery itself dates from 1208–14, during the time of King John, when other churchyards were closed by an Interdict of the Pope. Gilbert White, the Selborne naturalist, as a schoolboy at Basingstoke, went with some of his school-friends at night for a joke, and tried to blow up the Holy Ghost Chapel, but fortunately without much effect.

In New Street is the Willis Museum and Art Gallery, including many items of local historical interest, and a very good collection of clocks and watches. The Town Hall, 1832, is on the site of the former Mote Hall in the Market Place. The Municipal Offices are in a very pleasant Georgian house in London Road. To the south-west, on the corner of Southern Road and Victoria Street, is the Church of All Saints, 1915–18, by the well-known church architect, Temple Moore.

Only a mile or so east of Basingstoke's vast suburban development, but still managing to retain a countrified air, is the village of Basing. It has some pretty old cottages grouped round the church, and the huge remains of Basing House, famous as the toughest nut that Cromwell had to crack in the Civil war. Entering the ruins by an outer gate, the visitor crosses the disused Basingstoke Canal. Schemes are afoot to make this usable again. The Paulet family became owners

Nineteenth Century view of the gateway of Basing House

of Basing in 1428. Sir William Paulet, the first Marquess of Winchester, demolished the Norman motte and bailey castle, of which the huge circular bank remains. He erected in its place a magnificent red brick Tudor mansion. This became known as the 'Old House', after the building of a later extension known as the 'New House'. He received licence to crenellate (fortify) in 1531, and the building which he erected must have looked extremely fine. It was defended by several tall towers. He died in 1572, aged ninety-seven, and at the time of his death he had 103 descendants.

Basing House will always be famous for the long and trying siege which it underwent during the Civil War. John Paulet, the 6th Marquess of Winchester, proclaimed that he would defend Basing House to the end, even if it was the last stronghold remaining in Royalist hands. He gathered some soldiers together and they prepared themselves to withstand a long siege, if necessary. The siege did, indeed, last for two years and three months. In spite of the close investment by Waller, the Parliamentary General, he was unable to capture the house. Frequent sallies were made, causing many casualties on both sides. Finally, Cromwell himself took it by storm in October 1645. Among the prisoners was Inigo Jones, the famous architect. The great house was utterly destroyed, local people being invited to carry away as much stone as they needed. All that is left today is a fine piece of brick boundary wall with a tower at each end; one is a summer house and the other a dovecote. On the opposite side of the road from Basing House is Grange Farm, where there is a magnificent brick barn.

The very handsome church adjoins the ruins of Basing House. Originally a Norman building, the only Norman works remaining are the north and south arches of the tower; the rest is sixteenth-century Perpendicular and is almost entirely constructed of mellow old red brick. In a gable above the west window is a niche containing a statue of the Blessed Virgin and Child. The tradition is that the Puritans, when they ransacked Basing House, did not see this statue because it was concealed by a fortunate growth of ivy.

The church is large and spacious, with a fine old roof, the beams of which are supported by angel corbels. Of outstanding interest are the four Paulet tombs in the chancel, which balance each other, two on either side, each pair being separated by a doorway leading into the north and south chapels respectively. Those on the south side have beautiful Renaissance details. The north chapel has a coved plaster ceiling, and some unique wooden tracery in the windows. Some corbels on the north side bear coats of arms, among which may be distinguished the key of Paulet. The Royal Arms of Charles II is

Old print of Basing Church

dated 1660, the year of the Restoration of the Monarchy. In order to remind people that republicanism was at an end, all churches were ordered to display the Royal Arms. In the south chapel are numerous mural monuments to the Dukes of Bolton, including one by Flaxman, 1794, commemorating the 6th Duke. They were descended from the 5th Marquess of Winchester. The Jacobean pulpit was moved here from Basingstoke, a fact recorded in the church-wardens' accounts in 1622.

Sherborne St. John, just north of Basingstoke, seems to be awaiting the menacing advance of the new town, but at present is still a typical Hampshire village with a most interesting church. This contains many brasses to delight the brass rubber, as well as some fine monuments, notably an early sixteenth century one to Ralph and Edith Perall. Both hold hearts, and this usually means that they died when away from their home, only their hearts being buried in their own church. The brick porch is dated 1533, and over the inner doorway are the kneeling effigies of the donors of the porch, John Spiers and his wife. There is a unique Jacobean lectern with three sides, and a good Jacobean pulpit dated 1634. In the east window of the north aisle there is some sixteenth-century stained glass, and also one panel dated 1638.

A few miles north of Sherborne St. John is The Vyne, Hampshire's most beautiful stately home. It was the work of William, Lord Sandys, who was a remarkable man in that, for some thirty-one years, he managed to retain the favour of his sovereign, Henry VIII, and also

The Vyne
(South front)

his own head! He disagreed with Henry's treatment of Catherine of Aragon, and also with the Reformation, but was wise enough to keep his opinions to himself. He entertained Henry at The Vyne three times, Anne Boleyn, as Queen of England, was with him on one occasion. He was appointed Lord Chamberlain in 1526 and died in 1540. His son having pre-deceased him, he was succeeded by his grandson, William, third Lord Sandys, who enjoyed the property for sixty-seven years. He entertained Queen Elizabeth there in 1569.

During the siege of Basing House Waller, the Parliamentary General, quartered his troops at The Vyne. Tradition says that the magnificent stained glass in the Chapel was saved by being taken down and buried. The Civil War, having made considerable inroads into the family fortunes, caused William, the Sixth Lord, to sell The Vyne and retire into Mottisfont Abbey. The purchaser was a successful London barrister named Chaloner Chute. One of his most famous cases was his defence of Archbishop Laud. He was chosen Speaker of the only Parliament summoned by Richard Cromwell, son of Oliver.

The south front of The Vyne, by which the house is approached, is of beautiful old brickwork with a blue diaper pattern, and is early sixteenth century. The stone dressings round the windows are mid-seventeenth century, the sashes being later. The pair of stone eagles on either side of the front door was a present from Horace Walpole to his great friend John Chute, in 1745. The north front faces the lake. The most prominent feature is the Corinthian portico, the earliest example of its kind forming a part of any country house. Speaker Chaloner Chute employed John Webb, the disciple of Inigo Jones, to add it to the north front. It is of brick covered with stucco, but the pediment is of painted wood. The accounts submitted by Edward Marshall, the Master Mason, for this work still exist. At the east end of the north front is the Chapel, with Gothic windows and stone battlements, this is considered one of the most beautiful private chapels in England, and remains just as it was in William, Lord Sandys' day.

Visitors are asked to go first into the Stone Gallery, the west wing of the ground floor, formerly a dormitory for guests' retainers, then a greenhouse, and now a Sculpture Gallery. The wall tablets were another present from Horace Walpole to John Chute. The Stone Gallery leads into a series of drawing-rooms hung with Italian damask. These rooms have plaster ceilings of John Chute's design, and contain some good pictures, interesting furniture, some Chippendale and some earlier, a Tompion clock, and cases of china and glass. The large dining-room has a stone chimney-piece with caryatids and a classical frieze, possibly carved by Edward Marshall, and a set of Queen Anne walnut chairs.

From the dining-room a door leads into the Chapel Parlour, which has linen-fold panelling from the Sandys' time, and a John Chute rococo plaster ceiling. In it is a chamber organ by Henry Holland, 1788, brought from Osterley. The Ante-Chapel was developed in Strawberry Hill style by Horace Walpole and John Chute, who was an amateur architect of considerable skill. In the windows are some fragments of glass from the Holy Ghost Chapel at Basingstoke.

The glory of the Chapel itself is the magnificent Flemish glass in the three windows of the apse, equalled only by that of King's College Chapel, Cambridge. In the upper section of the southernmost window is Christ bearing His Cross and meeting St. Veronica, and in the lower section is Queen Margaret of Scotland, daughter of Henry VII, and her Patron Saint, St. Margaret. The central window has the Crucifixion above, and Henry VIII and his Patron Saint, Henry II of Bavaria, below, and the northern window has the Resurrection above, and Catherine of Aragon and her Patron Saint, St. Catherine, below. The date of this glass cannot be later than 1527, because it was in that year that Catherine of Aragon's status began to decline. In the drapery of the stools upon which the Queens are kneeling are pet dogs. A doorway in the south wall leads into the Tomb Chamber, which John Chute built to honour the memory of his distinguished ancestor, Speaker Chaloner Chute. There is a fine reclining figure of the Speaker in Carara marble; the sarcophagus was designed by John Chute and finished by Thomas Carter. The very beautiful stalls in the Chapel are richly carved and are in two tiers with a canopy over the upper one. The early sixteenth-century encaustic tiles were found in various parts of the grounds, and are thought to have been made at Antwerp by an Italian, Guido de Savino. One of the tiles has a portrait of the contemporary Duke of Urbino.

In the middle of the ground floor is the Staircase Hall, and beyond this the Print Room, which has prints formerly pasted on to the walls by Mrs. William Chute and her nieces, c. 1815, print-pasting having been a genteel occupation of those days. Beyond the Print Room is the Strawberry Parlour, often used by Horace Walpole.

One of the most remarkable features of the house is the staircase, designed by John Chute himself c. 1760, rather in the Palladian style. It is one of his most splendid achievements. It has beautifully carved Corinthian columns and balusters, and a very fine, moulded plaster ceiling. It rises gently from the centre of the hall, and branches off to right and left, leading into galleries. It was described, at the time of its construction, as 'theatric'. On the first floor is the Library, of a later date, probably 1830–40, but with another fine stone chimney-piece, believed to be by Marshall. It contains some Chute family portraits. Next to it is an ante-room, and beyond that the Tapestry Room, with a series of wonderful Soho Tapestries of oriental scenes, woven by John Vanderbank about 1720. There are also some good Georgian chairs and other interesting furniture. The Oak Gallery, above the Stone Gallery, has splendid linen-fold panelling, with coats of arms, crests, initials and other devices carved at the top and bottom of each panel. One is that of Bishop Fox, who died in 1528, and another the Cardinal's Hat of Cardinal Wolsey, who was made a Cardinal in 1515. The panelling, therefore, must almost certainly have been carved between those two dates. The classical marble chimney-piece, possibly another of Marshall's works, is in the style of John Webb and Inigo Jones. There are also some portrait busts, including Roman Emperors, Charles I and Oliver Cromwell.

Chaloner Chute built a couple of garden houses, one of which still survives. It is a charming domed building of red brick in the shape of a Greek cross, with four short arms of equal length.

In 1956, Sir Charles Chute bequeathed The Vyne to the National Trust. It is open from April to September, inclusive, on Wednesdays and Bank Holidays 11 a.m. to 6 p.m. and on Sundays 1 p.m to 6 p.m. The Chapel is open for public worship on the fourth Sunday in each month at 6.15 p.m., from April to September.

CHAPTER VI

The Hampshire Border

Some two miles north of The Vyne is Bramley, which has a church well worth visiting, containing both Norman and Early English work, with a Jacobean brick tower erected in 1636. The Brocas Chapel was added to the church in 1801 by Soane and contains a large monument by Carter to Bernard Brocas, 1777. Surmounting the chapel externally are large crests representing boars' heads. Inside there are extensive wall paintings, including one of the murder of Becket, thirteenth century, and a huge St. Christopher, late fifteenth century, showing mermaids in the water at his feet. The church is decorated with a masonry pattern with rose stems. There is much old woodwork, including fifteenth-century bench ends, and a handsome eighteenth-century west gallery. In the north window of the nave is some mid-fourteenth-century glass, and in the south transept some sixteenth-century Swiss glass. There are also some brasses, and two displays of the Royal Arms. One dates from 1660 and the other, a great rarity, has the arms of Charles I as Prince of Wales.

Two miles to the north of Bramley is Silchester, the site of the Roman city of Calleva Atrebatum. It began as a Belgic capital, ruled over by a king named Commius. His tribe of the Belgae, the Atrebates, lived in northern France, and after their conquest by Caesar in 57 B.C., Commius and some of the tribe emigrated to Britain. Coins issued by a later king, Eppilus, bear the word *CALLE* (Calleva). After the Roman conquest in A.D. 43, an earthwork, known as the Outer Earthwork, was constructed, enclosing an irregular septagon of 230 acres. A strange feature about this city is that the old Belgic (pre-Roman) defences were retained, rather than giving place to the usual Roman rectangular plan. The Roman chequer-board street plan, however, was adopted inside the city. Towards the end of the second century a bank and ditch were constructed, enclosing less land than the outer earth-work, and reducing the area of the city to 100 acres. Air photography shows the line of the streets continuing on the north side of the later defences. The wall was erected during the third century, the face of the bank being cut away in order to build it. This magnificent defensive work was 9 feet thick at the base and 7 feet thick at the top. It is built of flint, obtained locally, strengthened by bonding courses of limestone brought from north Wiltshire. It still retains a height of 12 feet in some places, but the original height was probably about 20 feet. There were four gates, the east and west being the more important, having two arches, one later blocked. Through these gates ran the main road from London to South Wales. The north and south gates had a single arch, and through them went traffic to Winchester in the south and Dorchester in Oxfordshire. The walls are 1½ miles in circumference. There are no buildings within the walls except the church and Manor farm, which adjoin each other on the site of the east gate. It therefore occurred to the Antiquaries of the nineteenth century that here was a marvellous opportunity to excavate an entire Roman city, free from all later buildings such as had grown up in York or Winchester. The Rev. J. G. Joyce began this task in 1864, on behalf of the second Duke of Wellington, the local landowner. He continued it until 1878. The Society of Antiquaries conducted a systematic excavation between 1890 and 1909, and a further excavation took place between 1954 and 1958. The whole area of the city has therefore been excavated, a plan made and photographs taken, and the site since returned to agricultural use. It would have been too vast a work to preserve such a large area.

It is difficult to imagine that these peaceful fields were once a busy Roman city, and fascinating to imagine what the city looked like. In the centre was the Forum, which consisted of a courtyard surrounded on three sides by shops and offices and on the fourth by the Basilica, a magnificent hall, where justice was dispensed. Supporting the super-structure were two rows of Corinthian columns. The Baths were a short distance to the south-east of the Forum, and offered hot baths followed by tepid baths and finally a cold plunge. The modern Turkish bath is on much the same lines. Immediately adjoining the Forum at the south-east corner a most sensational discovery was made, that of a Christian Church. This was in 1893, and the fact that it really was a Christian Church was confirmed in 1958. All that was left was the transeptal plan of the building and the platform upon which the altar had formerly stood. This church dates from the end of the fourth century, and is thus the very earliest church in the country. Eight centuries divided it in time from the building of the existing Silchester Church. This dates from the thirteenth century and contains much of interest. The chancel is richly painted with a masonry pattern and in each square are roses. Mr. E. Clive Rouse, F.S.A., the well known authority on medieval wall-painting, cleaned and restored the paintings with wonderful results. The lancet windows in the east end had been replaced by a large Perpendicular window. On either side of this are two half-blocked original lancets with their painting which is now revealed, having been blocked for many centuries. The south aisle has good Decorated windows with reticulated tracery, and in this aisle is a beautiful recumbent effigy of a lady, in a canopied recess. There is no chancel arch, but instead there is a Perpendicular screen decorated with angels with outspread wings. The Jacobean pulpit has a fine, domed sounding board.

Immediately to the north of the church is the Manor Farm. A short distance from here, and just outside the wall, is the Amphitheatre, now very much overgrown with trees and bushes. It was reached by a postern gate which pierced the wall at this point.

The rich hoard of finds from all over the city was taken to Reading Museum. They are wonderfully displayed, and illustrate every phase of life in a Romano-British city. There is also a small Museum, a short distance to the west of the city, containing a small but admirable collection of typical finds.

Three miles east of Silchester is Stratfield Saye, the seat of the Duke of Wellington. It was presented by the nation to the first Duke, as a token of personal esteem and gratitude for his many brilliant campaigns, culminating in the epic victory of Waterloo. At first he intended pulling down the mansion, but decided against it. The house, built in *c.* 1630 by Sir William Pitt, has Dutch gables terminating the wings. There are several rooms with rococo ceilings, *c.* 1720–60.

Near the mansion in the park is the church, a brick Classical building in the shape of a Greek cross, with a central dome. It contains some seventeenth-century monuments, notably one to Sir William Pitt and his wife, 1636, of fine workmanship and signed and dated by the sculptors, John and Matthew Christmas, 1640. 'Copenhagen', the first Duke's charger at Waterloo, was buried with full military honours when he died in 1825.

On Heckfield Heath on the road between Reading and Basingstoke, is a tall column surmounted by a statue of the first Duke. Heckfield church contains, among other interesting features, a great rarity, a small crusading money chest. All churches were ordered to provide one by Pope Innocent III in the early thirteenth century. In Heckfield churchyard is buried Neville Chamberlain, who was Prime Minister when war was declared in 1939. All his most sincere efforts to prevent war having failed, he resigned, and died a few months later.

Bramshill is situated in the north-east of the county, near the

Berkshire border. The magnificent house, built by William Lord Zouche, a friend of James I, on the site of an old castle, is now a Police College, not generally open to the public. It was to have been occupied by Prince Henry, son of James I, and the Prince of Wales's feathers and motto 'Ich Dien' are above the central pediment, but the Prince died before the house was quite ready for him. James I often stayed there, and planted some Scots pines in the park, introducing these trees for the first time into England.

A tragic event occurred in 1621, when Archbishop Abbot of Canterbury was staying there. When hunting in the park, he accidentally shot and killed a keeper instead of a dear at which he was aiming his cross-bow. So dreadfully did he feel this, that he went every year to Bramshill on the anniversary of the keeper's death, and spent the day in prayer and solemn meditation.

There is an imposing gateway, and a long avenue leading down to a lake and then up to the terrace on which the house stands. The Cope family purchased the house in the eighteenth century, and owned it until the twentieth century.

Near Bramshill, and right on the Berkshire border, is Eversley, where Charles Kingsley was Rector from 1842 until his death in 1875. He is probably best remembered now as the author of *The Water Babies*, written partly at the old Plough Inn, Itchen Abbas, where the River Itchen is supposed to have inspired the poem 'Clear and Cool'. This book is still often seen on children's bookshelves but, though it is in part a charming fairy story for children, it was also written as a 'Tract for the Times', showing up not only the chimney sweeps and their cruelty to the apprentices, but also the wealthy householders who tolerated such a state of affairs, as well as cruel schoolmasters and other offenders. It was obviously directed as much to adult as to child readers.

Westward Ho! is a spirited story of Elizabethan times, but many of Kingsley's books, such as *Alton Locke* and *Two Years Ago*, though ostensibly novels, were mainly vehicles for drawing attention to the shocking conditions of work at that time, and explaining the point of view of the Chartists and others, who were trying to remedy the abuses by political reform. With Frederick Denison Maurice and others, Kingsley was among the early Christian Socialists. They wanted to make the Church and all who called themselves Christians, more sensible of their Christian obligations towards the poor and oppressed, and also to show the aggrieved working people that votes and charters were not enough, but that Christian principles were necessary on their side too, before the state of affairs could really be remedied. The passing of the Chimney Sweepers Act in 1864 was partly brought about by the influence of *The Water Babies*, and other social reforms owed much to Kingsley and his friends.

St. Mary's Church at Eversley has only one old portion, being the south wall of the chancel. The rest was rebuilt in brick in 1735, and restored again after Kingsley's death as a memorial to him. There is a bas-relief to him in the north aisle, and his grave is on the south side of the churchyard, with a Maltese cross on which are enscribed the words, "God is Love'. On the chancel floor is a brass to Richard Pendilton, 1502, and in the archway between the chancel and north chapel a beautifully sculptured tomb inscribed, 'Dame Mariane Cope, MDCCCLXXII. May she rest in peace'.

Farnborough, in the far east of Hampshire, near both the Berkshire and Surrey borders, was mentioned in the Domesday Book as 'Fernberga', meaning Fern Hill, but its history goes even further back. It is thought to have been part of some land left by King Alfred to a nephew in 901, and in 951 it was acquired by Bishop Aelfsige of Winchester. At that time it was probably a tiny hamlet in heathy, pine-clad country. It is known to have had a church in the twelfth century, but even in 1850 the population was under 500. After the Crimean War, when it was decided that Britain needed large, permanent military establishments, Farnborough and neighbouring Aldershot were chosen, and soon grew into large towns.

The Royal Aircraft Establishment was first set up at Farnborough in 1906. It was originally called 'His Majesty's Balloon Factory', then 'The Army Aircraft Factory', next 'The Royal Aircraft Factory' and finally became known by its present name. It is now a vast centre for manufacture, design and research, training, and every aspect of aviation, and the Farnborough Air Show, first held in 1948, attracts people from all over the world. During the twentieth century, the population has increased to between 40,000 and 50,000.

Although Farnborough is now mainly a modern town, it still has some interesting historical buildings. The Parish Church of St. Peter dates from Norman times, though it has been much altered and enlarged. It has a very attractive, low tower and spire of timber. Parts of the nave wall are Norman, and a Norman doorway has been re-set in the wall of the modern south aisle. Some wall-paintings of St. Mary Magdalene, St. Agnes and St. Eugenia, believed to date from *c*. 1300, were discovered during alterations. There is a Jacobean screen and other seventeenth-century woodwork.

In the crypt are buried five Earls of Anglesey, whose country seat was Farnborough Park. It is believed that there was a house in Farnborough Park in Norman times. In Restoration times it was a hunting lodge. Nell Gwynne is thought to have stayed there, and later visitors included Sir Joshua Reynolds and David Garrick.

On Farnborough Hill stands a remarkable mansion, much timbered and pinnacled, built by the publisher, Longman, about 1860. It was bought by Eugénie, the tragic Empress of France, in 1883. She married the Emperor Napoleon III in 1853, and for a time they enjoyed the gay life of the Second Empire in Paris. Their son, the Prince Imperial, was born in 1856. The Franco-Prussian War, however, in which the French were heavily defeated at Sedan, and Napoleon III taken prisoner, brought the Empire to an end. Eugénie and her son escaped to England, where Napoleon later joined them at Chislehurst, but he only lived until 1873. In 1879 the Prince Imperial volunteered to serve with the British Army in the Zulu War, and was killed in a skirmish, fighting with great courage. The heartbroken Empress lived at Farnborough until 1920, when she died aged ninety-five. Her house is now a Convent School. In memory of her husband and son, she built St. Michael's Abbey. The church, which stands at the top of a wooded hill, is a fascinating building, designed by Gabriel Distailleur, in the most flamboyant Gothic style, with flying buttresses, pinnacles and gargoyles, and a dome similar to that of the Invalides in Paris. The tombs of Napoleon III and the Prince Imperial were transferred to the crypt in 1888, and the Empress Eugénie's tomb is between them. The crypt is open to the public in the afternoons only, but the church is open all day. The Abbey was first a Priory of Premonstratensians, but became a Benedictine Abbey in 1895. The monks, as well as their religious and educational duties, carry out beautiful book-binding. The Abbey also has an interesting museum of imperial souvenirs.

In Ship Lane is the very old Ship Inn, formerly called the 'Royal George', but altered to 'The Ship' after the sinking of the *Royal George* at Spithead. Another interesting inn sign is the 'Tumbledown Dick', probably named after Richard Cromwell.

Adjoining Farnborough to the south, practically without a break, is Aldershot. It was left, as was Farnborough, in King Alfred's will to his nephew. The district of Aldershot was, however, inhabited long before King Alfred's time. Just west of the town, in the Military Training Area, are two pre-Roman earthworks. One, with the intriguing name of Batt's Hog Stye, is approximately square, and encloses four mounds. The other is wrongly called Caesar's Camp. A collection of mesolithic flint implements was found there, so that it must have been inhabited hundreds of years before Julius Caesar set foot in Britain. Some gold coins from the seventh century were also found there. It is thought that King Alfred may have used the camp when

St. Michael's Abbey Church, Farnborough
(By kind permission of Farnborough Abbey)

he was fighting against the Danes near Farnham. At that time Aldershot was a tiny hamlet in the parish of Crondall. In about A.D. 976 King Edgar gave Crondall, including Aldershot, to the Monastery at Winchester, and it remained in Church hands until the Dissolution. Two years later, Henry VIII gave it to the Dean and Chapter of Winchester Cathedral. The land was taken by the Parliament during the Civil War, but was returned to Winchester Cathedral after the Restoration.

Aldershot Manor belonged from the sixteenth to eighteenth centuries to the Tichborne family, and there is an interesting document, the 'Crondall Customary' which gives the names of all the tenants of the Manor and their holdings at that time. The document may be seen in the Public Library. The present Manor House, now the Registrar's Office, in a park at the east end of the town, dates from 1670. At that time, and until the middle of the nineteenth century, Aldershot was a small village. What is now the very wide, built-up Farnborough Road, was a turnpike road running through lonely, heathy country, and much infested by highwaymen. Like Farnborough, Aldershot became a town at the time of the Crimean War. The land for a permanent Military Establishment was bought in 1853 and the first barracks, along what is now Wellington Avenue, were built in 1854. From that time, both military and civil Aldershot have increased at a tremendous pace. The old, depressing Victorian barracks have been, or are rapidly being, replaced by cheerful modern ones with every amenity. The town also has a modern shopping centre, car parks and open spaces and sports facilities. It has a little light industry, but is mainly residential.

The Parish Church of St. Michael the Archangel stands on Church Hill, near the Manor House. It was originally built in Norman times, but practically nothing of the old church remains. The Lady Chapel, formerly the chancel, is the oldest part and houses some interesting monuments to various Tichbornes, and an armorial brass to Sir John Whyte, 1573. The tower is seventeenth century, but the rest of the church has been much restored and enlarged. Nearby are the Heroes' Garden and Shrine, memorials of the two world wars. The Shrine has a large figure of Christ stilling the storm, made from a block of Portland stone said to have been rejected by Sir Christopher Wren when building St. Paul's Cathedral. There is also a rockery made of stones from the war-damaged buildings of other towns.

At the west end of the town, opposite the end of Wellington Avenue, is the Royal Garrison Church of All Saints, full of military history, with Colours and other relics of the campaigns of many wars,

Statue of the Duke of Wellington at Aldershot

Odiham, 'The Bury'

great and small. In the south porch is an iron-bound cross made of
timber from Bazentin, France, a memorial to those killed in action
in September 1916. Near this church, on a mound, is a fine equestrian
statue by Matthew Cotes Wyatt of the Duke of Wellington on his
favourite horse, 'Copenhagen'. It was erected in London in 1846, and
transferred to Aldershot in 1885.

The village of Crondall, to which Aldershot formerly belonged,
lies a few miles to the west. It has some very charming old houses,
and the Church of All Saints, though much restored at various times,
retains much magnificent Norman and Transition work from the
twelfth century, some good brasses and monuments, and many other
interesting features. The fine brick tower was built in mid-seventeenth
century.

Some ten miles west of Aldershot is Odiham (pronounced Odium),
a charming small town consisting mainly of one long street containing a large number of beautiful houses, many of them Georgian, but
some earlier. Among the finest is Marycourt, early eighteenth century,
with a beautiful shell porch. An open space to the south of the High
Street is known as The Bury. This contains more charming old
houses and the church, which is large and handsome, particularly the

Odiham Castle

tower, being of Jacobean brickwork. The pulpit and the west gallery are also of this period, as are the delightful almshouses which stand to the south of the church. There are various curious relics in the churchyard. At the south-west corner is a small lock-up known as the 'Pest House', and on the north side of the churchyard are the stocks and whipping-post. A great rarity, now preserved in the church, is a shelter for the parson's use at funerals, much resembling a sentry-box.

Odiham Castle is not in Odiham itself, but about a mile to the west of the town near the village of North Warnborough. The castle ruins stand in a very picturesque situation by the long disused Basingstoke Canal. The ruins consist of an octagonal tower of flint rubble, all the ashlar having been removed. The castle dates from the early thirteenth century, and in 1216 sustained a siege by Louis, Dauphin of France. During the next century, it was for long the prison of David, King of Scotland. The Castle is now in the guardianship of the Department of the Environment.

The village of North Warnborough contains many charming old cottages. The village of South Warnborough lies about three miles south of North Warnborough. The church is full of interest and contains work of all periods from Norman to Perpendicular. It has a 'Hampshire type' timber belfry. Timber was often used in churches as Hampshire had no stone quarries. There is some old heraldic glass and some good monuments, especially one to the White family, with effigies of the father, mother, fourteen sons and six daughters, 1570. Some of the children hold skulls, denoting that they predeceased their parents.

CHAPTER VII

Moving South

Alton is a pleasant old town towards the north-east of the county, surrounded by hop fields. The town of Alton, celebrated for its beer, has had a long history. When Henry I succeeded to the throne in 1100 his brother Robert rebelled against him, but soon peace was restored and a treaty between the two brothers was signed at Alton. Normandy Street is believed to commemorate this event. In the reign of Edward I Alton returned two members to Parliament.

The church, originally Norman, but much added to in the Perpendicular period, has a thrilling history. During the Civil War, in 1643, Waller, the Parliamentary general, was advancing from Surrey, in the hope of capturing Winchester. He surprised the Royalists at Alton, but the main body of them, under Lord Crawford, fought their way out and headed for Winchester, leaving Colonel Boles, with about eighty men, to fight a rearguard action. Having set the town, then largely thatch-roofed, alight, in the hope that the pungent smoke would check the parliamentary advance, they retired into the church, where they made a last stand. Colonel Boles was finally killed, having accounted for several of the enemy. Tradition says that he made his last stand in the pulpit. When Charles I heard of this action he said, 'Bring me a mourning scarf; I have lost my best officer'. He ordered a brass, recording the event, to be placed in Alton Church, and a similar one in Winchester Cathedral. Bullet marks are still to be seen, notably in the south door. The Norman church was originally cruciform and the crossing arches of this church still remain, the capitals of the arches being carved with various birds and beasts, which repay close inspection. In the fifteenth century a large new nave in the Perpendicular style was erected north of the Norman church, which lost its transepts and became part of the south aisle of the new church. The rough old font may possibly be Saxon. It is made of one huge block of stone. Cast out at the restoration of 1868, it was found at Cirencester, and having been bought back for £10, it was once more restored to the church. It stands upon a mill stone, representing Alton's paper industry. The Jacobean pulpit is one of the most beauti-

Alton, St. Lawrence Church

ful of its kind, but it has unfortunately lost its sounding board. On a pillar in the nave are paintings of St. Cornelius, King Henry VI and an archbishop.

Besides the beer and paper industries, various branches of the cloth trade flourished in Alton. At one time 500 persons were recorded as being employed in the making of barracan, a coarse kind of camlet or woolly material, and there were also serges, white yarns, tabinets, bombazines, ribbed druggets and other woven fabrics, in which a brisk trade was carried on with America. Silk was manufactured, as well as the coarser materials, and the festival of Bishop Blaise was celebrated in Alton until the nineteenth century.

Alton was also a great coaching town, lying on one of the main roads from London to the west. In about 1750, long before the establishment of fast coaches in the early nineteenth century, a coach known as the 'Alton Machine' travelled between Alton and London, starting at six o'clock in the morning and taking most of the day for the 50 miles. It went up to London three times a week, and returned on the alternate days, driven by E. Gilbert 'if God permits'. Passengers paid 10s. for inside seats, but probably much less for travelling in what appears, from an old advertisement, to be a large washing-basket strapped to the back of the coach.

William Curtis, the famous botanist, was born at Alton in 1746. He founded the *Botanical Magazine*. A descendant of his, another William Curtis, wrote the *History of Alton*, in 1896 a most admirable local history.

Alton has some fine old Georgian mansions, notably Westbrooke House, now the Council Offices, which contains some handsome fireplaces rescued from a demolished building. Among modern buildings, several are of outstanding beauty and interest. Alton Abbey, founded in 1885, some of the buildings of which are by Sir Charles Nicholson, belongs to the Anglican order of St. Paul. The Brothers' principal duty is to care for retired merchant seamen. In 1910, St. Mary's, Wantage established a branch here, especially to look after mentally deficient women. The buildings are in Turk Street, and the very beautiful chapel contains a magnificent reredos by W. D. Caroe.

The Curtis Museum, is open on weekdays from 2 p.m. to 5 p.m. Saturdays from 10 a.m. to 1 p.m. and 2 p.m. to 5 p.m. but closed Sundays, Wednesdays and Bank Holidays. This museum contains interesting collections of agricultural and brewing implements, and Victoriana. At the west end of the town is the famous Lord Mayor Treloar's Cripples' Hospital, and at the east end is Eggar's Grammar School, dating originally from the sixteenth century.

South of Alton, just off the main road to Winchester, is the village

The "Alton Machine"

Jane Austen's house at Chawton

of Chawton, sacred to the admirers of Jane Austen because the house there, where she lived for the last few years of her life with her mother and sister Cassandra, has been made into a Jane Austen Museum, open all the year round. Besides many interesting relics in the house, there is Jane's carriage in a shed in the garden. She lived all her life in Hampshire, except for a short period at Bath after her father's retirement. Of the two novels about Bath, one, *Northanger Abbey*, was written at Steventon, and the other, *Persuasion*, much later, at Chawton, though neither was published until after her death. *Northanger Abbey* is one of the most lighthearted, with the honest, good-hearted, unsophisticated heroine Catherine Morland, led into ridiculous ideas by the 'horrid' Gothic novels recommended by her flighty friend, Isabella Thorpe, until she imagined that the Tilneys' house, Northanger Abbey, would be a sort of Castle of Udolpho. The frivolous life of the visitors to Bath is delightfully drawn, and every character seems true to life, with the possible exception of General Tilney. As some early critics observed, he would hardly have sent a young girl home alone in a post-chaise, however much he had been disappointed in her lack of fortune. Jane was, however, very young when she wrote this book, and may be forgiven for this slight exaggeration. *Persuasion*, written nearer the end of Jane's life, is on the whole more serious, and Anne Elliott, the heroine, has far more depth of character, though the book has its share of amusing incidents and

ridiculous people such as Sir Walter Elliott. It also has the one drama-
tic incident which even Jane's non-admirers seem to remember, that
of Louisa Musgrove's fall from the Cobb at Lyme Regis.

Pride and Prejudice, written in the early days at Steventon, is a
great favourite. The very first sentence, 'It is a truth universally
acknowledged, that a single man in possession of a good fortune must
be in want of a wife' sets the key to the book and to much else
of Jane's writing. As a Victorian critic wrote, 'In satire, humour, wit
and irony, all of a refined and amiable character, she is excellent.'
Nearly all her characters are true to life indeed, Macauley and one
or two other critics compared her with Shakespeare in that respect. They
are neither perfectly good nor exceptionally bad and, although nothing
of great moment happens, all the little events seem interesting. Jane
Austen was the first novelist to make the commonplace events of
ordinary life quite uncommonly entertaining, and her admirers probably would not exchange her for all the other worthies of Hampshire.

Emma, the other novel written at Chawton, is considered the best
by many critics. Curiously enough, she only brought Hampshire into
one of the novels, *Mansfield Park*. The inimitable description of
Fanny Price's visit to her family in their squalid home at Portsmouth,
after years of living in the refined surroundings of Mansfield Park,
is one of the most vivid descriptions contained in her novels. The
bustling life of the naval port, and the Sunday walks on the ramparts
where Mrs. Price and the other naval and marine wives met to discuss
their unsatisfactory servants, all seem so real that one can picture oneself clearly in Portsmouth in Nelson's time. Jane's letters in general
were as racy and amusing as her novels. She lived at Chawton from
1809 until the last two months of her life, when she was sent to
Winchester, with Cassandra, to have the best medical attention. She
retained her sense of humour until the very end. In one of her last
letters, after blaming herself for complaining, she went on, 'You will
find Captain—— a very respectable, well-meaning man, without much
manner, his wife and sister all good humour and obligingness, and I
hope (since the fashion allows it) with rather longer petticoats than
last year.'

In another letter of about that date she wrote, 'Mr. Lyford [her
doctor] says he will cure me, and if he fails I shall draw up
a memorial and lay it before the Dean and Chapter, and have no
doubt of redress from that Pious, Learned and Disinterested Body.'
If her caustic wit occasionally verged on the unkind, her readers
would still forgive anything to a writer who could express herself so
cheerfully and amusingly within a week or two of her death.

Another Hampshire writer was Gilbert White, who lived most of his life at Selborne, about four miles south-east of Alton, on the Alton–Petersfield road. In this part of Hampshire there is a series of hills, on the Upper Greensand, facing eastwards. Some of them rise very steeply, are covered with beechwood, and known as hangers, and of these Selborne Hanger, with the charming village lying below it, is one of the most famous. Gilbert White was born at his grandfather's Vicarage in 1720. In 1730 Gilbert's father, a barrister, bought the house called The Wakes, and Gilbert lived there, at intervals, until the end of his life. His grandmother, who lived to a great age, was interested in natural history, and encouraged Gilbert to study it. He went to school at Basingstoke, and to college at Oriel, Oxford, where he became a Fellow. While at Oxford, he won an important literary prize, and was presented by the poet Alexander Pope with a copy of his translation of Homer's Iliad and Odyssey. White was ordained in 1747, and became Curate of Selborne in 1751, with other curacies in the district. From time to time he spent some months at Oxford, but the greater part of his life was spent at 'The Wakes', where he continued to live after his father's death.

He never married, but had a great many nephews and nieces, great-nephews and great-nieces, in whom he took the utmost interest. One of his nephews, Jack, son of Gilbert's brother John, was educated by Gilbert, and lived with him at Selborne for some time, and Jack's mother also lived at The Wakes after her husband died. Other well-known inhabitants were Thomas, Gilbert's faithful servant, and the beloved tortoise, Timothy. The famous *Natural History of Selborne* was published in 1789, only four years before Gilbert White's death, but he was collecting material for it all through his life at Selborne, making notes in his journal, and writing long letters to his family, friends and many other naturalists. He noted minutely every bird, plant, animal, reptile and insect, and every detail of the weather. He described how one little bird, having accidentally built its nest in too sunny a position, spent the whole day hovering over the nest to shelter the nestlings from the sun, and White himself would devote equal time, trouble and, if necessary, self-sacrifice, to make his observations, or to help his neighbours. He was a clever gardener, and he did much for the village in the way of improving roads and pathways and planting trees. He made a path up the Hanger called 'The Bostal', and his brother John, another clergyman and naturalist, helped to make the zigzag path which some people find easier.

Gilbert took a tremendous interest in all the people in his parish, was a constant and most welcome visitor, and gave useful hints on crop-growing, brewing, and every possible concern. He worked out that, by using rushlights instead of candles, people could have eleven hours' light for the price of two hours', and he told the housewives how to make the rushlights. He noted that most people lived in 'good stone and brick cottages, which are glazed, and have chambers above stairs'. Some of these cottages still stand in the village. He also noted that the women were able to supplement their husbands' incomes by spinning wool, 'for the making of barragons, a genteel corded stuff manufactured at Alton'. This may have been the same as the 'barracan' made in Alton in the previous century, but perhaps it had acquired greater 'gentility' in the meantime. He felt satisfaction at the increase in the consumption of vegetables. 'Common farmers', he wrote, 'provide plenty of beans, peas and greens for their hinds [labourers] to eat with their bacon, and those few who do not are despised for their sordid parsimony. Potatoes have prevailed . . . within these twenty years only, and are much esteemed by the poor, who would scarce have ventured to taste them in the last reign' [that of George II]. A woman whom he visited once covered his bacon with sugar, saying that nothing less was good enough for him. In 1784, when he heard that a balloon flight was to be made by a Mr. Blanchard from London, he worked out, quite scientifically, what time the balloon might pass over Selborne, and then went all round the village, and out into the fields, to tell everyone about it, so that nobody missed the remarkable spectacle.

He noted all the old customs and superstitions of the village, and also kept meticulous accounts, so that altogether a most accurate account of Hampshire village life at that time may be obtained from his writings. The impression given of himself is that of a most kind and considerate pastor, relation and friend, with considerable humour and a great zest for life. He took a great interest in the antiquities of the district, as well as in the natural history.

Gilbert White died in 1793, and by his own wish was carried to his grave by six honest labourers, 'respect being had to such as have raised up large families': the bearers were given 10s. each 'for their trouble', a very good sum in those days. His humble grave in Selborne churchyard has a headstone marked simply. 'G. W. 26th June 1793'.

Selborne Church, though considerably restored at various times, contains some Norman and Early English work. The tower is probably fifteenth century. There is a beautiful, comparatively modern, memorial window to Gilbert White in the south aisle. It shows St. Francis of Assisi, surrounded by many of the birds and animals mentioned in the *Natural History*. Over the altar there is a Flemish Tryptych of the 'Adoration of the Magi' by Jan Mostaert, presented by Gilbert White's brother Benjamin. In the churchyard is another interesting grave, that of 'The Trumpeter' who, in the early nineteenth

The Rodney Monument in Old Alresford Church

century, rallied the villagers with his trumpet in some anti-tithe riots, in which the poorhouse was attacked. There is a huge yew tree, much loved by Gilbert White, and believed to be well over 1,000 years old.

Outside the churchyard is the 'Plestor' (Saxon Play-place) and on the opposite side of this is The Wakes. This is now a Gilbert White Museum, given by a warm admirer, Mr. Robert Oates. A relation of Mr. Oates was Captain Lawrence Oates, the 'very gallant gentleman' of Scott's Antarctic expedition in 1912, and there is an Oates room at The Wakes with relics of this expedition.

There was formerly a priory of Augustinian Canons, about one mile north-east of Selborne, founded by Bishop Peter de Rupibus in 1233. It was almost entirely destroyed, but has lately been excavated, and many interesting discoveries made, including the ground plan, largely by the Rev. George Knopp, the late Rector of Worldham.

Yet another writer in this part of Hampshire was Mary Russell Mitford, of Alresford, whose best known work, *Our Village*, brings the village people to life rather as Jane Austen's works did with the upper middle classes. Miss Mitford admired Jane's work on the whole, particularly *Emma*, but seems to have considered Jane herself rather forward and flirtatious. While Jane wrote mainly for her own and other peoples' pleasure, Mary Russell Mitford had to do it for money, her father being a spendthrift. She was born at 27 Broad Street, New Alresford, in 1787.

Alresford belonged to the Bishops of Winchester from quite early times. Bishop de Lucy (1189–1204) built a dam on the Itchen, between Old and New Alresford, intending to make the Itchen navigable from Alresford to Southampton. A reservoir of 200 acres was made by the dam, but only 60 acres of it now remain. In the seventeenth and eighteenth centuries the town was several times destroyed by fires. After the last one, in 1736, it was almost entirely rebuilt in the early Georgian style, so that it is a town of very great charm. Broad Street leads down to the bridge across the dam, and the village of Old Alresford is on the other side. It has an eighteenth-century church, in which is a handsome monument to Admiral Lord Rodney and his wife.

CHAPTER VIII

The Itchen Valley

A pretty route from Alresford to Winchester runs along the Itchen valley, passing through Itchen Abbas, where Kingsley stayed at The Plough. Avington, across the river, has an extremely good Classical Church, 1768–71, with all the fittings of the period, mainly made of mahogany said to have been taken from a Spanish prize. North of the altar is the tomb of Margaret, Marchioness of Caernarvon, who paid for the rebuilding of the church, but died before it was finished.

Avington Park has a fine red-brick mansion, now flats, where Charles II used to stay. The Dukes of Buckingham owned the estate for a time. Cobbett condemned the Duke of his time for game laws and other offences, but had to admit that his turnip-hoers were some of the prettiest, tallest and most cheerful girls he had ever met on his 'Rural Rides', so that the Duke must have been a good employer.

The Itchen Valley road leads into Winchester from the north. Another way goes south from Alresford through Tichborne and Cheriton, and approaches Winchester from the east. Tichborne is a pretty village with some sixteenth- and seventeenth-century timber-framed cottages. The 'Tichborne Dole' of a gallon of flour given to the villagers dates from 1150. It is said that Lady Mabel Tichborne, on her deathbed, begged her husband to give a dole to the poor, and he heartlessly agreed to give the value of the land which she could go round while holding a flaming torch. The gallant lady rose from her sick-bed, and succeeded in staggering round 23 acres. She prophesied that, if at any time the dole was not given, a family of seven sons of Tichbornes would be succeeded by a family of seven daughters, and the line would die out and the house fall. This did in fact happen, when in 1794, the magistrates stopped the dole. It was soon re-introduced, and has continued until this day. The Church of St. Andrew, on a hill above the village, has a Saxon and Norman 'Overlap' chancel and some other Saxon and Norman work, a fifteenth-century doorway and staircase to the roof-loft, some Elizabethan and Jacobean woodwork, and a brick tower of 1703. The north aisle, separated from the church by an iron railing, belongs to the Tich-

Avington Church

borne family, who have always been Roman Catholics. It contains their family monuments.

Cheriton's Church of St. Michael has an Early English nave and chancel, a tower rebuilt after a fire in 1744, and a seventeenth-century altar table. The Battle of Cheriton, in 1644, was one of the decisive actions of the Civil War. The Royalist forces under Lord Hopton were encamped on the north side of Cheriton Down, and the Parliamentarians under Waller were on Hinton Ampner Ridge. The Royalists were defeated, with very heavy casualties, and the way to Winchester and the west was left open to the Parliamentarians.

The road eastward from Cheriton to Winchester runs over a beautiful area of Downland, the highest point being Cheesefoot Head at the top of Telegraph Hill, from which there is a glorious view, southward to the Isle of Wight, south-west over Southampton and the New Forest, and northward to the Berkshire Downs. Below Cheesefoot Head on the north is a natural amphitheatre or Devil's Punch Bowl, much smaller than its namesake at Hindhead, Surrey, but quite as beautiful.

South of the road is St. Catherine's Hill, a rounded Down with a clump of beeches on top. It is not very high, but, standing up above the Itchen valley, it forms a landmark in the Winchester district. The famous archaeologist C. F. C. Hawkes believes that there was an unfortified settlement there c. 550–450 B.C., with some habitations and

The upper waters of the River Itchen at Cheriton

storage pits. About 250–200 B.C. the hill was fortified by Iron Age people, with deep ditches and high banks. It was re-fortified about 150–100 B.C., and more advanced Iron Age people lived there. Hand-made pottery and objects made of bronze and antler-horn were found there during excavations.

At Worthy Down, north of Winchester, pottery made with a primitive wheel was discovered, and there were also human skeletons and bones of horses, cows, sheep, pigs and two breeds of dog. Currency Bars, an early form of money, were also in use there.

About 50 B.C. the district was invaded by the Belgae, refugees from Gaul, driven out by the Romans. They destroyed the defences of St. Catherine's Hill by fire, and after this the site was deserted for hundreds of years. The Belgae were more advanced people, with good iron tools, including a heavy wheeled plough, and they used coins. They settled themselves more in the valleys than on the hill tops, and the first settlement on the site of modern Winchester probably dates from about this time. This was the first place above Southampton where the Itchen could be forded. Commius, the Chieftain or King of the Belgae made his capital at Silchester.

The Romans captured Winchester from the Belgae about A.D. 43 and named it Venta Belgarum. Coins of Claudius, Nero, and other Roman emperors have been found there, and it was an important road centre. After the Romans left Britain, Winchester was occupied by the Saxons under Cerdic, and in 519 he made it the capital of Wessex. A small church was built in 634, when Bishop Birinus converted King Cynegils to Christianity. The first Cathedral was built c.650, and in 674 the Bishopric of Dorchester in Oxfordshire was transferred to Winchester. In the ninth century, when King Egbert of Wessex became the first King of England, he kept Winchester as his capital. St. Swithun, Patron Saint of Winchester, was Bishop from 852–62, and built a great wall round the Cathedral. This saved it when the rest of the city was destroyed by the Danes in 860. The legend of St. Swithun is that, being a humble man, he wished to be buried outside the Cathedral, and when his wishes were disregarded at his death, he caused rain to fall for forty days to express his wrath. Hence the superstition, 'St. Swithun's day if it shall rain, for forty days it will again'. St. Swithun's day is 15th July.

Alfred came to the throne in 871, and eventually defeated the Danes. He built schools, encouraged art and literature, instituted the *Anglo-Saxon Chronicle*, founded a large Nunnery with a church called the Nunnaminster, and instructed his son Edward the Elder to build a new Minister beside the Saxon Cathedral. The site of these three buildings has been excavated.

St. Catherine's Hill and the River Itchen near Winchester

After the Norman Conquest, William the Conqueror made London and Winchester joint capitals, and was crowned in both. He built a large castle by the Westgate, one of the original city gates, and a large palace where the Butter Cross now stands, but this was destroyed by fire during the war between Stephen and Matilda, 1141, and only one pillar of it now remains, in a passage leading from High Street to the Square and thence to the Cathedral. In the Square is the Museum, in which are interesting finds from all periods of Winchester's long history. The Normans, under Bishop Walkelyn, also built the transepts of the present Cathedral, in a plain style. The tower is later, and in a richer style. Bishop de Lucy, who built the dam at Alresford, extended the north choir of the Cathedral eastward, and was responsible for the Early English work east of the great screen, and for part of the Lady Chapel. Bishop Edington demolished the west towers and is believed to have designed the present west front, though the upper part of this was by the celebrated William of Wykeham who was Bishop from 1367 to 1404. William of Wykeham also rebuilt the magnificent nave, one of the largest in Europe, in Perpendicular style. In the north aisle there is a splendid Norman font of black Tournai marble, carved with scenes from the life of St. Nicholas of Myra, the original Santa Claus. A memorial tablet, brass and window to Jane Austen are also in the north aisle. Wykeham's chantry is in the south aisle, with three monks kneeling at his feet. There are many other interesting and beautiful chantries and tombs, including that of William Rufus, and above the presbytery screens are some mortuary chests, supposed to contain the bones or other relics of kings from Cynegils to Canute. There are some wall paintings in the north transept, Norman and Tudor roof-bosses, carved stalls and misericord seats, and a glorious fifteenth-century screen, with well restored figures of bishops, saints and martyrs, and a crucifix in the middle. The west window is made up of fragments of old glass from various parts of the Cathedral, and there is more old glass in the east window and the Lady Chapel. In the south transept there is a window to Izaac Walton 'the Compleat Angler', who lived in the Close towards the end of his life, and fished in the Itchen and Test, and among very many other objects of beauty or interest is a figure, in the retro-choir, by Sir Charles Wheeler, 1962, of William Walker the diver. Between the years 1905 and 1912 the east end of the Cathedral was in danger of collapse, owing to changes in the water-level under it, and it had to be underpinned at very great trouble and expense, much of the work being done by William Walker, who often had to work actually under water, so that we owe to him, as well as to the many Bishops and

Winchester Cathedral and Deanery

others who built the Cathedral, the preservation of one of England's most beautiful and historic buildings.

Among many interesting events that took place in the Cathedral were the marriages of Henry IV, 1403, and of Mary Tudor to Philip of Spain, 1554.

William of Wykeham was also responsible for the building of Winchester College and New College, Oxford.

The beautiful houses in the Close include the Deanery, part thirteenth and part fifteenth century, the Pilgrims' School, a late seventeenth-century brick mansion with the very fine thirteenth-century Pilgrims' Hall adjoining. This has a hammer-beam roof with kings and queens carved on the ends of the beams, Number 10 has a thirteenth-century vaulted undercroft, and Cheyney Court is a very good Tudor building with barge-board gables. Just outside the Close gate is St. Swithun's Street, in which a battle took place between the forces of Henry III and the rebel Simon de Montfort. Parts of the old city wall survive round about here, and the King's Gate, leading from St. Swithun's Street into College Street, is one

Kingsgate, Winchester

of the old city gates. Above it is the tiny church of St. Swithun-upon-Kingsgate, dating partly from the fifteenth century.

The house in College Street, in which Jane Austen died, is marked by a tablet.

The College is built on the lines of the Oxford and Cambridge Colleges. Dedicated to St. Mary, it has a beautiful statue of the Virgin and Child over the gate. The Chapel has been much restored, but retains some original fan-tracery wooden ceilings. There are two main quadrangles in the Perpendicular style, and near the Chapel is a fine Wren building known as 'School'. Near the entrance to the old kitchen is a painting of a curious emblematic figure, part man and part animal, known as 'The Trusty Servant'. There are cloisters where the scholars used to take exercise, and a conduit under an open porch where they used to wash. The beautiful modern cloisters, by Sir Herbert Baker, opening into Kingsgate Street, are a Memorial to Wykehamists killed in World War I. The College, now one of our most famous public schools, was originally founded, in 1382, for 'seventy poor and needy scholars'. There are guided tours, except on Wednesday and Sunday mornings at 10 a.m. and 11.45 a.m., and 2 p.m. and 3 p.m., and, in April-September only, at 4.30 p.m.

Winchester College

Wolvesey Castle, Winchester

Farther along College Street, on the Left, is the Bishop's Palace, Wolvesey, designed by Wren, and the ruins of Wolvesey Castle, built by Bishop Henri de Blois in the early twelfth century, but largely destroyed in the Civil War. One of the best remaining sections of the old City Wall is nearby. There is a pleasant walk outside the wall, along the bank of the Itchen, leading to the eighteenth-century City Bridge. St. Swithun had earlier built a bridge on this site. The City Mill, a charming old house near the bridge, now a youth hostel, belonged to the Abbess of Wherwell before the Dissolution. It was then taken as Crown Property, but Queen Mary I presented it to the citizens of Winchester after her marriage to Philip of Spain in the Cathedral. Another charming timbered house, Old Chesil Rectory, in Chesil Street just across the bridge, now a restaurant, is believed to be the oldest house in Winchester.

In the Broadway, west of the City Bridge, is a fine statue of King Alfred, by Hamo Thorneycroft, erected in 1901, the millenary of Alfred's death. On the left are the eighteenth-century Abbey House, the Mayor's official residence, and the Victorian Guildhall, and on the right St. John's Hospital, an almshouse founded by John Devenishe in 1275. The chapel is thirteenth century, the other buildings Victorian.

Broadway leads into High Street. On the left is a colonnade called The Pentice, under which are both old and modern shops. Beyond this, the fifteenth-century Butter Cross retains one original statue, though much of it was restored in Victorian times. Behind it is another good timbered house. Farther up is the old Guildhall dating from 1713, now used by Lloyds Bank. Over the door is a statue of Queen Anne, and a handsome clock overhanging the street. Opposite is God-Begot House, with a restored front but fifteenth-century side in Royal Oak Passage. At the top of the street is the Westgate, mainly thirteenth century, but with a fourteenth-century west face with two early gun-ports. The lower part was formerly a debtors' prison. Over the gate there is a museum, which contains a set of Tudor standard weights and measures. From the roof there is a fine view over Winchester. St. Giles's Hill can be seen in the background, together with St. Catherine's Hill.

All that remains of the Norman Castle, near the Westgate, is the Great Hall, a fine building with arcades with Purbeck marble columns. On one wall hangs the so-called 'King Arthur's Round Table', now believed to be thirteenth century. Recent excavations revealed the plan of the old keep of the castle, which was over 50 feet square and had walls 16 feet thick. Henry III was the last King to be born in the castle. During the Civil War, when Waller's forces had taken most

Statue of King Alfred, Winchester

of the city, the castle held out for a long time, but was finally captured by the Parliamentary forces, and nearly all destroyed. Not far from the Westgate on the other side is the Plague Stone, where country people used to leave food during the great plague of 1666, and the townspeople left their money in a bowl of vinegar to disinfect it.

Charles II, who loved Winchester, planned to build himself a magnificent palace on the site of the old castle on the west hill. Sir Christopher Wren designed it, and it was begun, but Charles' death prevented its completion. The royal family took no further interest in it, and it became a barracks until in 1895 it was destroyed by fire.

About a mile south of Winchester is St. Cross Hospital, an almshouse founded in 1133 by Bishop Henri de Blois, brother of King Stephen, for thirteen poor men, and added to in the fifteenth century by Cardinal Beaufort, who founded an 'Order of Noble Poverty'. The brethern of Bishop de Blois' foundation wear black gowns and caps, and those of Cardinal Beaufort's foundation have plum-coloured gowns and caps. St. Cross is the oldest almshouse in Britain, and is one of the most beautiful groups of buildings anywhere. In the outer courtyard there is a very old brewhouse. The inner quadrangle is entered by the gatehouse or Beaufort Tower, under which is the Porter's Lodge, where the old custom of a 'Wayfarer's Dole' of bread and beer has been kept up ever since Norman times. Any genuine traveller may have it, until the day's ration is finished. There is a

Winchester Westgate from the east

The Beaufort Tower and the Brethren's Hall, Hospital of St. Cross,
Winchester

St. Cross Church and the chimneys of the Brethren's lodgings

figure of Cardinal Beaufort in a niche over the inner side of the gateway. On the north side of the inner quadrangle is the great hall, on the west the very picturesque houses of the brethren, and on the east an ambulatory or covered walk, with an infirmary gallery above. In the south-east corner is the very beautiful cruciform Chapel of St. Cross. The choir and transepts are Norman, and the rest of the building rather later. It contains some medieval glass and wall paintings, three brasses, a late Norman font and many other points of interest.

St. Bartholomew's Church, Hyde, towards the north end of Winchester, is also partly Norman, and was formerly associated with Hyde Abbey. The Abbey had been founded by King Alfred, and his grave is believed to be somewhere in this part of Winchester. Nearby is a fifteenth-century gatehouse.

The Normans, who seem to have been insatiable church builders, also built a cruciform church dedicated to St. Catherine, on the hill which took its name from this church, but it was completely destroyed after the Dissolution. On the top of a hill is a 'miz-maze', similar to that at Breamore, possibly cut by a Wykehamist in the early eighteenth century.

Winchester, besides being at one time an important wool town and a centre of religion and education over the centuries, is also a military city, and there are some very interesting Regimental Museums in Southgate Street and Romsey Road. The modern, industrial part of

Hursley

Winchester lies mainly east of the Itchen, and is hardly seen from the old city. A great many books have been written about Winchester, and many more could be written without ever exhausting the interest of this glorious and historical city.

About five miles south-west of Winchester is Hursley, a charming village with an old forge and some medieval cottages. John Keble was Hursley's famous and beloved vicar, from 1835 for about thirty years, and many of the cottages date from his time. He was born at Fairford, Gloucestershire, where his father was Vicar, but his mother was a Ringwood girl, so that he was half Hampshire by birth. He was educated by his father until he was fifteen, when he won a scholarship to Corpus Christi College, Oxford. When only eighteen, he won a 'Double First' in Classics and Mathematics, a distinction previously held only by Sir Robert Peel. He also won various literary prizes. Like Gilbert White, he became a Fellow of Oriel and, also like him, combined for a time the academic with the pastoral life. He was ordained in 1815, and at times helped his father at Fairford. While there, he wrote most of *The Christian Year*, that 'best-seller' book of poems for all the Sundays and other Christian festivals throughout the year, which went into 150 editions in his lifetime. Included in it are some of our well known hymns such as 'New Every Morning'. His Oxford pupils loved him for his kindness and sense of humour, as well as respecting him for his learning. He was made Professor of Poetry at Oxford, but became more famous for his part in the 'Oxford Movement', or 'Tractarian Movement.' He and his Oxford friends, Newman, Pusey and others, felt strongly that the Church had lost its place in the life of the country and that religion had become dry and uninspiring. They wrote a series of 'Tracts for the Times' from which the movement took its name. They aroused much controversy and regrettable disputes between High and Low Church, but they certainly succeeded in bringing the Church to life, and brought about perhaps the greatest religious revival since the time of John Wesley.

In 1835 Sir William Heathcote, the excellent squire of Hursley, who had been one of Keble's Oxford pupils, presented him to the Hursley living. He was an ideal parish priest, concerning himself with every detail of his parishioners' lives. He and his wife, with the Heathcotes and the Yonges of Otterbourne, built schools and churches, including those of Otterbourne and Ampfield. Hursley Church was rebuilt in Gothic style on the site of an old Georgian one. The old tower was retained, and Sir William Heathcote added a spire to complete the Gothic effect, but about 100 years later it was found to be unsafe and had to be demolished. The windows illustrate the

Scriptures from the Creation to the Day of Judgement. One shows the unfortunate Job covered with boils.

Keble's wife helped him in everything. At the end of her life she became an invalid, and they retired to Bournemouth, where they died within a few weeks of each other in 1866.

An earlier inhabitant of Hursley was Richard Cromwell, son of Oliver. He married Miss Major of Hursley Park and made his home there. Oliver Cromwell stayed there with him. Richard very reluctantly accepted the office of Lord Protector of the Commonwealth at his father's death. He was a kind, honest and deeply religious man, but lacked resolution and ambition, and was quite unsuited to his high office. He was jokingly, and rather unkindly, known as 'Tumbledown Dick'. At the Restoration, he was thankful to live abroad. Eventually he returned to England where he died in 1712 aged eighty-six, and was buried at Hursley. There is a monument in the church to the Cromwells, and a cross in the chancel floor to John Keble.

At the north end of Hursley Park is Merdon Castle. It was originally an Iron Age stronghold, the huge entrenchments of which were converted into a castle by the indefatigable Henri de Blois. It was very short-lived, being occupied for only about thirty years during the mid-thirteenth century. The principal remains, besides the huge earthworks, are the gateway, now reduced to a shapeless mass of flint rubble from which the ashlar has been stripped, and a very deep well.

One of John Keble's most ardent collaborators was Charlotte Yonge, of Otterbourne, the famous Victorian novelist. Otterbourne is two or three miles from Hursley on the Winchester–Southampton road, and Charlotte lived there with her parents, to whom she was devoted. Her religion was the mainspring of her life, and second only to duty to God came absolute obedience to her parents. This ideal comes out in many of her novels. *The Heir of Redclyffe* was published in 1853 and brought her instant fame, but she had been writing, and having her work published, from the age of fifteen. Her first printed work, *Le Chateau de Melville*, was written in 1838 to raise money for a Church School, and all her profits were given to school and church building and to missionary work. *The Heir of Redclyffe*, over which Jo, in *Little Women*, was found crying in an attic, provided a Mission Schooner. *The Daisy Chain*, published in the same year as *The Heir of Redclyffe*, and *The Pillars of the House* are perhaps the best of her fascinating books about large Victorian families. The spreading of religion was her over-riding concern but, as one of her biographers noted, 'she made goodness attractive' and, because she had a very real gift for story telling, and in general managed to make her characters quite natural, she was the ideal novelist for the time in which she lived. Her historical novels are well worked out, and she was very careful to have her facts as correct as possible, but the Victorian family novels are the ones that have survived, and in which one seems to be living with the families while reading the books.

Curiously enough, though she was very well educated and genuinely in sympathy with the poor, doing all that she could for them in a personal way, she did not seem interested in schemes for permanent reforms, wage raising, or tackling poverty on a large scale. Indeed, Rachel Curtis in *The Clever Women of the Family* and Theodora Martindale in *Heartease*, who did have advanced ideas, seem to have been intended to excite the readers' disapproval. Charlotte disliked Kingsley's Christian Socialism though he, on the other hand, admired her books. She undoubtedly had a strong influence over her readers. She was born in 1823, and died in 1901, two months after Queen Victoria's death, so that she may be considered to be the very essence of Victorianism.

CHAPTER IX

The Meon Valley

South of the Winchester–Petersfield road, and east of the Winchester–Southampton road, there is beautiful downland country interspersed with woods. Several lovely old villages lie in the Meon Valley in this south-east part of Hampshire. East Meon, at the upper end of the river, is a charming village with a beautiful Norman church, All Saints, standing high up above the village, with a background of green downlands. It includes Norman doors and windows, an enriched Norman tower with a rather later spire, and one of those magnificent. Tournai marble fonts, of which Hampshire has four out of the seven in England. This one shows the Creation and the Fall of Man, the expulsion from Paradise, and Adam learning to dig and Eve to spin. There are some good modern windows, the east window of the chancel being by Comper in memory of the 1914–18 war. Across the road from the church is a fifteenth-century Court House, now a private residence.

West Meon was the birthplace of Thomas Lord, of Lord's cricket ground fame. The inn sign commemorates him, and he is buried in the churchyard. Richard Cobden, the nineteenth-century Radical, also lived in West Meon as a boy. The Church of St. John the Evangelist is good Gothic Revival, and has a Jacobean altar table.

Warnford, a little further down the Meon, has a church standing in a park. It has Latin inscriptions on the north wall and the south wall under the porch, saying that the original church at Warnford was founded by Wilfrid of York, perhaps the first Christian missionary to this part of England, and that the church was rebuilt by Adam de Port, an ancestor of the St. Johns family. It has a Saxon sundial, a massive Norman tower, and a Norman nave with rather later windows, a late twelfth-century Purbeck marble font, some fifteenth-century misericord seats in the chancel, old benches, perhaps sixteenth century, in the nave, seventeenth-century screen, pulpits and altar table, monuments to the Neale family, and a Royal Arms of George IV, 1821. Near the church are the ruins of an old Manor House, dating from about the time of King John. It is wrongly called King John's

East Meon

Warnford Church

House, but it actually belonged to the St. Johns. The remains are those of an arcaded great hall with three bays, a buttery and a kitchen. One tall pillar remains to its full height of 25 feet.

Charles II, during his escape after the battle of Worcester, passed through Warnford, where his supporter, Colonel Gunter, was awaiting him. Gunter, for fear of calling attention to the King, pretended not to recognise him, and they met a little later on Old Winchester Hill, an Iron Age Stronghold, where they could talk safely. They spent the night at the house of Gunter's married sister, Mrs. Symons, near Hambledon, where Charles pretended to be a Roundhead, and reproved some of the company for swearing. Nobody suspected who he was, and the next day he resumed his journey to Brighton, whence he made good his escape to France.

Hambledon, besides coming thus briefly into English history, and having a very interesting church with some Saxon and some Norman work and many other noteworthy features, is famous for its cricketing traditions. Cricket was played on Broadhalfpenny Down at least as long ago as 1750, a fact which is recorded on a stone near the Bat and Ball Inn. The inn sign shows the quaint old bats and the dress worn by cricketers at that time. The Hambledon Club was the first to draw up a set of regular rules for the game of cricket, in 1774. The ground is still in use.

Meonstoke has a church, St. Andrew, with Early English chancel and nave arcades, a Purbeck marble font, c. 1200, a seventeenth-century German carving of Jacob wrestling with the angel, and other interesting features. Old Winchester Hill, where Charles II and Colonel Gunter met, lies just to the east of it, and has a single bank and ditch, and three round barrows. The prehistoric ridgeway, running from the Wiltshire to the Sussex borders, passes through the middle of the camp.

Corhampton, just across the river from Meonstoke, has a most interesting Saxon church, probably dating from the early eleventh century. The 'long-and-short' work and the pilaster strips of the exterior, the north doorway, chancel arch, a stone chair in the chancel, a sundial similar to that at Warnford, and the bell openings at the west end, are probably all of this early date. The font is Norman, south door and windows Early English and pulpit Jacobean. There are some remains of wall paintings. The east end of the chancel was unfortunately rebuilt in poor brickwork.

At Droxford, just down the valley from Meonstoke, Winston Churchill, the War Cabinet and the Allied Chiefs used the railway station as a headquarters before the D-Day operations in June 1944.

The Church of St. Mary and All Saints, though largely restored in the nineteenth century, has some features of all the architectural periods from Norman to Jacobean, and a 1935 screen by Sir Charles Nicholson. In the south chapel there is a graceful thirteenth-century figure of the mother of John Droxford. Izaac Walton used to stay at the Rectory and fish in the Meon.

Wickham was the birthplace of William of Wykeham in 1324. It is an attractive little town with a very wide Market Street and many charming houses, dating from Tudor until modern times, the Church of St. Nicholas was very much restored in 1862, and the west tower and spire are of that date, but there is a Norman doorway with the badge of King Stephen on one of the capitals, and in the south transept is a fine monument, 1615, to Sir William Uvedale with his wife and children. Chesapeake Mill, in the street leading to the church, is believed to have been constructed from timbers of the American ship *Chesapeake* after her defeat by the British frigate *Shannon*.

Bishop's Waltham, a few miles west of the Meon Valley, is another of Hampshire's remarkably historical towns. It is known to have been inhabited in the Bronze Age, the remains of pit dwellings, pottery and flint implements and other relics having been found. In recent times, the 'Wessex Bell Barrow' was found and excavated in Shore Lane, not very far from the town centre. The Roman road from

Bishop's Waltham Palace

Winchester passed through Bishop's Waltham, and Roman coins from the first to the third centuries have been found there, with other Roman relics. The Saxons also had a large settlement there, and in King Alfred's time 'Wealdham' or 'Wealtham' as it was then called, was the administrative centre of a 'Hundred' (a division of land able to support about a hundred families).

In 904 King Edward the Elder, who owned land at Waltham, exchanged it with the Bishop of Winchester for some land at Portchester. Hence the addition of 'Bishop's' to the name. In 1001 the town was destroyed by the Danes, but it was soon built up again, and at the Domesday Survey in 1086 it had at least three mills and two chapels. In 1136, the busy Bishop Henri de Blois built himself a fortified palace within a deer park, and other Bishops resided there and entertained many royal visitors. Henry II held a council there in 1182 to organise a crusade. Richard Coeur de Lion stayed there after his coronation at Winchester, and before he started on his last crusade. William of Wykeham often resided there, and he built the great hall. He died there in 1404. Henry V visited the Palace in 1415, the year of Agincourt, and Henry VIII in 1532, before crossing to France for the 'Field of the Cloth of Gold'.

Courts Baron and Courts Leet were held in the Palace twice a year until the Civil War, when it was besieged by the Parliamentary forces and very seriously damaged. Bishop Curll, a Royalist, is said to have escaped in a dung-cart. For many years, nothing was done to repair the palace, and it deteriorated steadily, but eventually it was partly restored as a private residence. It is now owned by the Department of the Environment, and it is open to the public from March to April, weekdays 9.30 a.m. to 5.30 p.m., Sundays 2.00 p.m. to 5.30 p.m.; from May to September, weekdays 9.30 a.m. to 7.00 p.m., Sundays 2.00 p.m. to 7.00 p.m.; November to February weekdays from 9.30 a.m. to 4.00 p.m., Sundays from 2.00 p.m. to 4.00 p.m. It is closed on these days between 1.00 p.m. and 2.00 p.m. and does not open on Mondays, except Bank Holidays. The chief remains are the front of the Great Hall, with five windows, part of a tower, some of the old domestic buildings, and the foundations of an apsidal chapel. Bishop Langton, 1501, built a brick wall round the site, and parts of this also remain.

In the town there are several good Georgian houses, including Barclays Bank, Pondside House, Roke Farm, and the Mill House with the old water mill with its grindstone still in the grounds. The Church of St. Peter was very much restored in the nineteenth century, but has a Norman font, a sixteenth-century tower, a very fine Elizabethan or early Jacobean pulpit, seventeenth-century altar rails and altar table, the 'Ashton Aisle' also seventeenth century but with a thirteenth-century arcade and a bust to William Ashton, 1629, and an eighteenth-century west gallery officially reserved for the occupants of certain houses. About half a mile out of the town along Coppice Road is Waltham Mill, a very old building on the site of one of those mentioned in the Domesday Book.

Farther down the Hamble River is Botley, centre of the strawberry-growing district of Hampshire. From very early summer until autumn, strawberries are sold at stalls by the sides of the main roads. Botley is a small town consisting of one main street with some handsome old houses and a Market Hall, 1848, with portico supported on four large piers of Portland stone, and a clock tower, added in 1897 to commemorate the Diamond Jubilee. William Cobbett, one of Hampshire's most colourful characters, owned Fairthorn Farm, Botley, and another house which no longer exists. He was born just outside the county, at Farnham, Surrey in 1762 but spent much of his life in Hampshire, and started on some of his Rural Rides from Budd's Farm, Burghclere.

In his youth he worked as a farm labourer, but took every opportunity to acquire education, and spent every spare penny on books. At the age of twenty he thought of joining the Navy, and tried to enlist on board the *Pegasus* at Portsmouth. The captain, who was a kindly man, and evidently thought that young Cobbett was trying to escape from some girl whom he had got into trouble, dissuaded him. 'He told me', Cobbett wrote, 'that it would be better to be led to church in a halter, to be tied to a girl that I did not like, than to be tied to the gangway, or, as the sailors call it, married to Miss Roper.' Instead, he joined the army and went to Nova Scotia, where he did so well that he soon became a sergeant-major. He married a sergeant's daughter, and their marriage was extremely happy. They had several children, and Cobbett was a devoted father. His wife was much beloved in Botley. His life alternated for some time between England and America. He was always passionately devoted to trying to remedy abuses. He wrote and edited papers under the name of 'Peter Porcupine', and for many years he published the *Political Register*. Among his 'Aunt Sallies', besides the paper money and the game laws already mentioned, were the 'Rotten Boroughs', the burden of taxation, 'follies' in the form of sham ruins in stone or cut out in yew or box, and the harshness of the penal laws. These were, in fact, greatly in need of reform. People could be hanged for picking a pocket or committing over 200 other offences. Curiously enough, one of Cobbet's butts was

William Cobbett

Sir Robert Peel, although it was during his time as Home Secretary that the number of capital offences was reduced to three.

In 1809, Cobbett protested most strongly in the *Political Register* against savage sentences of flogging imposed on some soldiers who had mutinied at Ely. Naturally mutiny could not be allowed to go unchecked, but the conditions in the army were such that people had considerable sympathy with the soldiers, and the sentences were shockingly brutal. Cobbett expressed himself in such violent terms that the government brought a libel action against him, and he was convicted and sentenced to two years' imprisonment and a fine of £1,000. His wife and children were allowed to visit him in prison, and to take him fruit and flowers from his farm and garden, and when he returned to Botley he had a triumphal progress. He never altogether recovered from the financial loss, but his sufferings were not in vain, as acts to abolish flogging in the army were introduced both in England and America not very long afterwards.

At one time Cobbett was M.P. for Oldham, and was able to make his voice heard effectively in Parliament. The 'Rural Rides', undertaken between 1821 and 1835 to obtain a complete picture of country life in England, involved his riding about forty miles a day, usually accompanied by one of his sons, and keeping a journal of everything that he saw and heard. The picture of the extreme poverty of many parts of the country is horrifying, but the style of writing is most entertaining. With his son George, Cobbett spent one night at Lyndhurst, on the way between Andover and Botley, and they had to sleep in a room leading out of another room. In the morning, they felt embarrassed at having to pass through the outer room, 'where, by possibility there might be a lady actually *in bed*; here lay I, my bones aching with lying in bed, my stomach growling for victuals, imprisoned by my modesty. But at last I grew impatient for, modesty here or modesty there, I was not to be penned up and starved, so . . . I thrusted George out a little before me into the other room, and through we pushed, previously resolving of course, not to look towards *the bed* that was there. But as the devil would have it, just as I was about the middle of the room, I, like Lot's wife, turned my head! All that I shall say is, first, that the consequences that befell her did not befall me, and, second, that I advise those who are likely to be hungry in the morning not to sleep in *inner rooms*: or, if they do, to take some bread and cheese in their pockets.'

He disapproved of public schools and colleges, describing those educated at them as 'those frivolous idiots turned out from Winchester or Westminster school, or from any of those dens of dunces called

The Hamble river

colleges and universities' and thinking more highly of himself as a self-educated man.

Tea was another of his targets. He described vagabonds who went round the country-side with tea-licences in their pockets. 'They wend *tea, drugs and religious tracts.* The first to bring the body into a debilitated state: the second to finish the corporeal part of the business; and the third to prepare the spirit for its separation from the clay.'

In general he found more for disapproval than for approval on the 'Rural Rides', but when he did find anything pleasing, he was glad to mention it. He spoke very highly of a Mr. Chamberlayne, of Netley, at one time M.P. for Southampton, who, when most employers of agricultural labour had lowered the wages gradually from 13s. (65p) a week to 7s. (35p) or even 6s. (30p), continued to pay his men the 13s. (65p). Another person who earned his approval was Mrs. Mears, a farmer's wife of Durley, near Botley, who plaited straw for hats and bonnets from the local dog's tail grass, and employed two girls in this work, paying them each 6s. (30p) a week. The plaited straw was sold to a milliner in Fareham.

In addition to the *Rural Rides* and many other publications, he produced *Cobbett's Parliamentary Debates* which were the forerunners of the present *Hansard*. The Freedom of the Press was another of his favourite causes. He was a man whom some people disliked intensely, and others liked and admired with equal intensity, but nobody could ignore him. He was frequently intolerant, and often conceited and hot-tempered, but at heart he was a kindly and most lovable man.

The Hamble River below Botley is one of those yachtsmens' paradises with which Hampshire is so richly favoured, and there is some yacht building at Bursledon and other places on the river, which runs out into Southampton Water between Hamble and Warsash.

CHAPTER X

South Hampshire

About three miles east of Warsash is the old town of Titchfield, an oasis of the picturesque in a mainly industrial landscape. The town is situated in a valley, through which the River Meon runs to the sea. The main street contains a number of old houses, mostly Georgian, though some are older. It is an historic old place, and owing to the Abbey and its situation on the busy road from Southampton to Portsmouth, it has been visited by a number of Monarchs. The church contains the earliest piece of church architecture in the county, the west porch, the lower part of the tower and the south-west angle of the nave, which have been dated as being of the seventh century. Except for these portions, the church has been rebuilt in a number of styles. It is entered by a good Norman door with chevron mouldings. The chancel was rebuilt in the thirteenth century and the south chapel in the fourteenth. The north aisle of the nave is good Perpendicular work of the fifteenth century. Unfortunately the south aisle of the nave, formerly Norman, was replaced by Victorian Gothic Revival work.

In the south chapel is the gorgeous tomb of the first Earl and Countess of Southampton and their son the second earl, with their effigies, with the husband and son on either side of the Countess. The Earl is wearing his robes of state with the Order of the Garter round his neck. On the north side of the monument are two small kneeling figures representing the third Earl, patron of Shakespeare, and his sister, and on the south side two daughters of the first Earl. This magnificent tomb is constructed of marble and alabaster in the Renaissance style. There is a tall obelisk at each corner. The monument was made in accordance with the will of the second Earl, who directed that monuments should be set up consisting of 'portraitures of white alabaster or such like one for my Lorde my father and my Ladye my mother, the other for mee'. It was the work of Gerard Johnson, a Flemish refugee. The deed of covenant of its construction is dated 6th May 1594.

Quite a different type of memorial is the charming little sculpture commemorating Lady Marie Wriothesley, who died in 1615 at the age

Titchfield

of four. It was executed by Epiphanus Evensham, a noted sculptor of the period. Another memorial of note is that to the Hornby family with recumbent effigy by Chantry, 1836. In the chancel is a fine monument to William Chamberlaine with effigies of himself, his wife and children.

About one mile to the north of the little town is the Abbey. This was one of Premonstratensian Canons, the Order originating in Prémontré, northern France. It was founded by Peter des Roches, Bishop of Winchester, in 1232. At the Dissolution the Abbey was surrendered to Henry VIII who, by letters patent dated 30th December 1537, granted the 'site, circuit and precinct' of the Abbey to Thomas Wriothesley, whose gorgeous tomb is in the Parish Church. In 1547 he was created Earl of Southampton for services rendered, especially in connection with the King's divorce from Catherine of Aragon. He then proceeded to convert the Abbey into a magnificent country house to be known as Place House, derived from Palace House. He demolished everything that was no longer necessary, in particular the tower, chancel and transepts of the Abbey Church. Their foundations have been excavated and marked out on the ground. The nave was converted into a Tudor residence, with splendid brick chimneys and crow-stepped gables, at what was formerly the west end of the church. Through the middle of the nave was driven a great gateway of a very imposing kind. This was the entrance to the Cloister Court, which was converted into the courtyard of the mansion. The

Saxon Tower of Titchfield Church

Monastic Frater or Dining Hall was on the north side of the court-yard. In what was the north walk of the Cloister Court are some medieval tiles of the late thirteenth or early fourteenth century. The majority of them show birds and beasts, but some are heraldic, such as castles for Eleanor of Castile, Queen of Edward I. Near the entrance to the Frater there is a Latin motto, each letter of which is on a separate tile. It may be freely translated, 'When you sit down to dine, remember the poor'. In the east walk of the Cloisters is the triple-arched entrance to the Chapter-House which, though blocked, is otherwise perfect.

Various historical events took place here. During the Civil War Charles I, who had escaped from Hampton Court where he had been imprisoned by Parliament, fled to Titchfield. From there he sent two of his Grooms of the Bedchamber, Colonel Ashburnham and Colonel Legge, to negotiate with Colonel Hammond, the Parliamentary Gover-nor of the Isle of Wight, with a view to re-starting the war and regaining his throne. For some reason the two gentlemen thought that Hammond would be won over to the King's side. Unfortunately for Charles, Hammond felt honour bound to serve Parliament, and told the King that he must consider himself a prisoner at Carisbrooke.

On the death of the fourth Earl of Southampton without male issue, the Titchfield estate passed to a daughter, Elizabeth who married Edward Noel. From the Noels the house passed again in the female line to the Dukes of Beaufort. One member of this family sold it in 1741 to the family of Delme. In 1781 the east wing was demol-ished, and after that the house gradually fell into ruin. It is now in the care of the Department of the Environment.

Fareham is an old town at the head of a creek which forms the western branch of Portsmouth Harbour. It is now a very up-to-date, partly residential and part industrial town. The very modern West Street is the principal shopping centre. The original High Street, which runs north from West Street, is a practically untouched Georgian street containing many delightful bow windowed houses. At the north end is the Parish Church, an interesting building of many dates and styles. At the north-east angle of the Early English chancel is some Saxon 'long-and-short' work. This old chancel became a north chapel to a new chancel built in 1888 to the design of Sir Reginald Bloom-field. The old nave was entirely destroyed in 1812 and what is des-cribed as a 'huge barn-like structure' was erected in its place. This in turn was entirely rebuilt by Sir Charles Nicholson in 1931. The eighteenth-century brick tower is surmounted by a charming cupola.

At the west end of the town, beyond the railway, is Bishopwood, now the episcopal residence of the Diocese of Portsmouth. It is a

Fareham High Street

delightful 'cottage ornée' with verandahs and 'Gothick' windows, and is the only episcopal residence with a thatched roof!

Portchester Castle, between Fareham and Portsmouth, is the westernmost of a chain of fortresses which the Romans erected to keep out Saxon barbarian pirates and other unpleasant people. These forts were placed at intervals along the east and south coasts from the Wash to Portchester. Archaeological evidence has established that they were erected during the last quarter of the third century. They were placed under the command of an official known as the 'Count of the Saxon Shore'. Hence the forts themselves are usually known as the Saxon Shore Forts. In Roman times, according to the 'Notitia Dignitatum' (a list of officials in the Empire), Portchester Castle was known as 'Portus Adurni'. At about this time Diocletian was ruling the Roman Empire which, at this period of its history, was beginning to be menaced by various enemies along its far-flung borders. When Diocletian became Emperor in A.D. 284, he appointed Carausius, a Belgic seaman of humble origin, to command the Roman fleet in the Channel. In 286 he appointed Maximian as his co-regent. Carausius, having been summoned to Rome, revolted and set himself up as Emperor with Boulogne as his headquarters. For some reason, possibly bad weather, or a defeat at the hands of Carausius, Diocletian and Maximum made peace with Carausius and recognised him. For seven years he ruled the waves in the Channel and the 'British Empire', until he was murdered by one of his officers named Alectus, who usurped his place. Alectus reigned for three years, after which he was defeated by the Emperor Constantius Chlorus, who restored Britain to Roman rule. One theory about the forts of the Saxon Shore is that they were built by Carausius, to be a defence against the Roman forces who were anxious to reconquer Britain.

The Roman fort of Portchester Castle is laid out in a square form, each side being approximately 200 yards, and the area 9 acres. The wall is 18 feet in height and is in remarkably good preservation; it is built of flint with bonding courses of stone and red tile. At intervals the walls were strengthened by bastions, of which fourteen of the original twenty remain. There are two main gates, east and west, each gate being exactly in the middle of its wall. There were two postern gates in the middle of the north and south sides respectively. A moat ran round three sides outside the walls, and the harbour provided a defence on the east side. After the departure of the Romans, for more than eight centuries the old fortress remained derelict until, in the twelfth century, the Normans converted it into a mighty stronghold, so strong that only Corfe and Dover could be compared with it. The main purpose of the modernisation of the Roman fort was to provide a

The keep of Portchester Castle, from the south east

fortified embarkation point in case war should break out with France, as happened so frequently during the medieval period. During the time of Henry I, 1130–5, the Roman walls were repaired and the gates rebuilt, and a strong keep was erected in the north-west corner of the fort. In *c.* 1170 the keep was heightened by one storey, so that it could command the whole fortress. The Normans also constructed an Inner Bailey, defended by a wall, bank and ditch, thus cutting off the remainder of the old Roman fort, which became the Outer Bailey. At the south-east corner of this, an Augustinian Priory was founded by Henry I in 1133, with a very beautiful Norman church which still remains. However, the Canons of the Priory objected to the constant noise of the garrison, and moved out to Southwick on the north side of Portsdown, where they re-established themselves in a remote and peaceful spot.

The visitor usually enters the Castle by the Land (or West) Gate, and then passes through the inner gate to the Inner Bailey. This gateway dates from three periods, the outer portion late fourteenth century, middle portion early fourteenth century, and inner portion twelfth century. The Watergate, or East Gate, has early Norman stonework in it. At the north-east corner of the Inner Bailey is Assheton's Tower, dating from the fourteenth century. Assheton was once a Constable of the Castle. At the foot of the keep are the remains of the Chapel, by way of which the staircase to the keep is gained. There is a fine view from the top; Portsdown to the north, Portsmouth Harbour to the east and south.

During the passing centuries, kings came and went, while some royal and other distinguished people were imprisoned at Portchester. Richard II, in 1396, built a palace against the south wall of the Inner Bailey. The ruins of the Great Hall, with a noble staircase leading up into it, still remain. Unfortunately Richard did not live to see it completed. Henry Bolingbroke rebelled against him and overthrew him in 1399. When Richard was deposed, and later murdered at Pontefract Castle in Yorkshire, Bolingbroke succeeded him as Henry IV. In 1441 the castle is described as 'ruinous and feeble'. Thereafter Portchester lost much of its former importance and became just a military depot and store-house. Henry VIII and later Elizabeth I were the last two monarchs to visit it. During the wars of the eighteenth century, a great many prisoners of war were confined in the castle, and numerous inscriptions which they carved are still to be seen. In 1793 the housing of all these prisoners became an urgent problem, which was solved by the erection of timber hutments in the Outer Bailey. In 1926 the Castle was presented to the nation by its owner, Mr. A. Thistlethwaite, and it is now in the care of the Department of the Environment. An excellent guidebook, with plans, is on sale at the castle. Excavations have been conducted in the Outer Bailey under the leadership of Professor Barry Cunliffe, resulting in some most interesting discoveries and increasing our knowledge of the past.

The church, formerly the church of the Augustinian Priory but now parochial, is a very excellent example of the late Norman style. It was formerly cruciform, but the south transept has been destroyed. The monastic buildings were formerly joined to the church on the south side; all that is left being the chutes which emptied the Rere-Dorter (sanitary conveniences). In the church are a huge Norman font, and two displays of the Royal Arms, those of Elizabeth I and Queen Anne.

While Porchester was important from the third century onwards, Portsmouth, grew up only very gradually. At first there was a small settlement round a creek called the Camber. Gosport was a small fishing village across the harbour, and is said to have been called 'God's Port' by Bishop de Blois, when he took refuge from a storm there in 1150. By the time of Richard I, Portsmouth had grown enough in importance to be granted a Charter in 1194. King John built the first docks there. The town was sacked and burned by the

French in 1338 and 1369, but it was gradually developing as a naval base, and it became more difficult to attack. Henry VII enlarged the docks, and Henry VIII enlarged them again, to an area of six acres. He also built Southsea Castle, one of the chain of forts stretching from Kent to Cornwall. Other Tudor fortifications which remain are the Round Tower and the Square Tower. From the Round Tower, a 'mightie chaine of Yron' as Leland described it, stretched across the harbour to Gosport at a cost of £40. There is a bust of Charles I, by the Channel Islands sculptor Le Sueur, presented by Charles as Prince of Wales in 1635, on his safe return from France and Spain in search of a wife.

George Villiers, Duke of Buckingham, favourite of Charles I, was assassinated by a dissatisfied officer named Felton, outside a house then known as Spotted Dog House, but now as Buckingham House, in High Street. Villiers had been unpopular for some time, because the King lavished too many favours upon him, and his unpopularity was increased by his failure to relieve a Protestant force at La Rochelle. Felton was hanged on Southsea Common, but many people felt that he had done a useful deed. The house in High Street is marked by a plaque.

In the Civil War, Sir George Goring held the town for a time for the King. The Parliamentary forces pressed him closely, and he was obliged to surrender, but not until he had obtained honourable terms by threatening to blow up the powder magazine in the Square Tower and so destroy most of the old town.

A happy event was the arrival of Katherine of Braganza. She disembarked at the Sally Port, an old gate on which is written, 'Heroes innumerable have embarked to fight their country's battles'. Katherine's marriage to Charles II took place in the Governor's House, formerly the 'Domus Dei', a religious foundation of Peter de Rupibus (or des Roches). Although, like other royal marriages, this was a political arrangement, in spite of Charles's many lady friends, the marriage was fundamentally happy. In Victorian times, the Governor's House became the Garrison Church. Charles II employed a Dutch engineer, Sir Bernard de Gomme, to add many fortifications, including ramparts all round the town. Portsea, north of the town, and Gosport were also fortified. Some of these old fortifications, including the Long Curtain and the King's Bastion, remain at the harbour end of Portsmouth High Street, though many were demolished in the nineteenth century. De Gomme also remodelled Southsea Castle, which consists of a square keep in a courtyard, surrounded by a curtain wall and dry moat. It is now a Museum, illustrating Portsmouth's history. It has the Royal Arms of Charles II over the gateway.

Daniel Defoe, writing of Portsmouth a little later, was tremend-
ously impressed by the fortifications, and by the prosperity of the
town. ' 'Tis evident', he wrote 'that the greatest fleet of sheeps that
ever were in the hands of one Nation at a time, would not pretend,
if they had not an Army also on Shoar ... to force their entrance into
the Harbour at Portsmouth.' Little could he imagine the destruction
which would come from the air two or three centuries later. 'The
business of the Navy is so much increased and so much of it is always
done here', he added, 'that it may be said that there is as much to
do in Portsmouth in time of Peace as ... in time of war, and more
too.'

In 1712, Jonas Hanway was born in Portsmouth. He invented that
admirable implement, the umbrella, which, at the time, met with
much ridicule. He also founded a Marine Society for helping street-
boys to become seamen, promoted street paving, and collected £7,500
for greatcoats for soldiers in the Seven Years' War. He hated tea-
drinking, whist, and female education, and was considered rather
odd, but undoubtedly benefited not only Portsmouth, but much of the
world.

In 1757 Admiral Byng was executed on his own quarter-deck in
Portsmouth harbour, because he had lost Minorca.

John Pounds was born in Portsmouth in 1766. Like Hanway, he
took a great interest in the poor street-boys. He was a shipwright in
the dockyards, but became a cripple, and took up cobbling instead.
He gave food, which he could ill afford, to the poor boys, and taught
them to read the Bible and to write on old bills or any odd scraps of
paper. In 1773 George III visited the town and held a Naval
Review. He gave money to the poor, and released prisoners confined
for debt.

A tragic event in 1782 was the loss of the *Royal George*. She was
in dock for repairs, with her portholes open. A sudden squall heeled
her over, water poured in through the portholes, and the ship sank
immediately. 'It was supposed', wrote the Portsmouth historian Lake
Allen in 1817, 'that between 900 and 1,000 passed, with this awful
suddenness, into a future state, with all their imperfections on their
heads.' Among them was Admiral Kempenfelt, the inventor of flag-
signalling.

Nelson seems to have been first at Portsmouth in 1776, when he
joined the *Worcester* as 4th Lieutenant. He had joined the Navy at
the age of thirteen, going straight to the ship without any preliminary
training, and in after years he was always very kind to the young
midshipmen, who adored him, as did all his officers and men. His
uncle, Captain Suckling, was Comptroller of the Navy, and likely to

become M.P. for Portsmouth, so young Nelson was fêted and given dinner by the Mayor, but his success in the Navy was due entirely to his own hard work, and in no way to influence.

After doing well in the West Indies, and then suffering a bad attack of yellow fever, he returned to Portsmouth, and was appointed to command the *Albemarle* when he was only twenty-three or twenty-four, one of the youngest Captains ever known. He went to Newfoundland for eight months, and when he returned, the entire ship's company volunteered to serve under him again, a great compliment, as this was just before the Mutiny at Spithead. The Mutiny, in 1797, was brought about by many grievances, uneatable food, brutal discipline, and miserable pay, which had not been increased since the time of Charles II. Nelson spent some time in London trying to secure redress for these grievances, and soon afterwards, Lord Howe brought to Portsmouth the news of an act of Parliament to improve conditions. Nelson sailed again from Portsmouth in 1801, before the Battle of Copenhagen, and in 1803 he embarked in the *Victory* for the Mediterranean, where he skirmished with the French for two years. He returned to Portsmouth in August 1805, spent a few weeks ashore, and then embarked again in the *Victory* for his last voyage. He had breakfast at the George, and waved from the windows to a vast crowd. The landlord then let him out by the back door and conducted him to Southsea Common, where he embarked, to the cheers of another great crowd. He

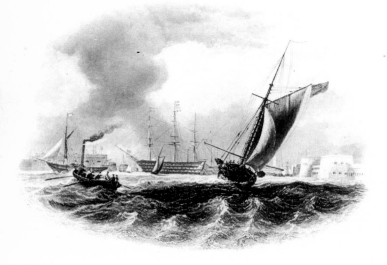

Shipping in the mouth of Portsmouth harbour (19th Century)

was then at the height of his popularity, and his death at Trafalgar was considered the greatest tragedy that could have befallen the nation.

The *Victory* had been launched at Chatham in 1765 (the second of her name, the first dating from 1560). She was the flagship of many admirals, but in 1797–1803 she was used as a prison hulk at Chatham. Nelson saw her there, and had her refitted. She was forty years old at Trafalgar, and was condemned to be broken up the next year, but was fortunately reprieved. She has been flagship to all the admirals in command at Portsmouth for a century and a half. For many years she remained afloat in Portsmouth Harbour, but in 1922 she was moved into dry dock and completely restored, and may now be visited on any weekday between 10.30 a.m. and 5.30 p.m. and on Sundays from 1 p.m. to 5 p.m. Her anchor is on the beach near Clarence Pier, Southsea, and there is a statue of Nelson in Pembroke Road.

Across the road is the Victory Museum, containing many items of naval interest, including models and figureheads, and a panorama of the Battle of Trafalgar by W. L. Wyllie, R.A. Other buildings of interest in the dockyard are the Semaphore Tower, in which is incorporated the old Lion Gate, dating from 1777. The Unicorn Gate, 1778, was moved in 1873 to mark the entrance to the dockyard extension. Also to be seen is the Navigation School with a dome,

Portsmouth Cathedral

1732, and a terrace of Georgian houses, long Row, *c.* 1717, now dockyard offices. St. Ann's Church, parish church of the dockyard, 1785–6, was damaged by bombs, but well restored in 1955–6. It has a beautiful ceiling, a Royal Arms possibly from an admiral's barge, and a modern window, 'Christ Ascendant over the Dockyard', showing the dockyard as it was after the war. The docks now cover 300 acres and are the largest in the world. Only H.M.S. *Victory*, the Victory Museum and St. Ann's Church are open to the public.

Portsmouth Cathedral, St. Thomas of Canterbury, is in many different architectural styles. The chancel is good Early English, *c.* 1180, and the transepts a little later. In the north transept there is a wall painting of the Last Judgment, *c.* 1250, restored by Professor Tristram in 1939. The church was severely damaged in the Civil War, and at the Restoration the nave was rebuilt in the Classical style, and a west tower added to take the place of the former central one. The tower has a dome and cupola, and a fine new ship weathervane, the old one, of 1710, having been blown down and now kept inside the church. The church became the Cathedral when the diocese of Portsmouth was separated from that of Winchester in 1927. Sir Charles Nicholson designed an enlargement in Gothic style. The old nave became the choir, and a new nave to the west of the tower made the tower central again, and new transepts were added. The Navy Aisle, commemorating naval history, incorporates the stained glass windows of the old south aisle of 1693, and has other windows showing people prominent in Portsmouth history. Unfortunately World War II prevented Sir Charles Nicholson's work from being finished. There is a monument to George Villiers, Duke of Buckingham, believed to be by Nicholas Stone, a noted sculptor of Stuart times, and many other interesting features. The Cathedral is to be completed in modern, late twentieth-century, style, so that it will form quite an architectural history.

There are some pleasant seventeenth-century houses, some with Dutch gables, near the Cathedral. In St. George's Road is the Landport Gate, 1760, believed to be the work of Hawksmoor, who designed the towers of Westminster Abbey. It is the last surviving gateway of old Portsmouth, and now leads only into a sports ground.

Across the ferry, in Gosport, is Haslar Royal Naval Hospital, a handsome George II building, with every modern improvement, but retaining most of the old work. Holy Trinity Church, not far away, dates partly from 169(and in it is an organ, once the property of the Duke of Chandos, of Canon's Park, Middlesex, which Handel used when composing.

The famous engineer of the Great Western Railway, Isambard

Kingdom Brunel, was born in Portsmouth in 1806, and in 1812 Charles Dickens was born at 393 Commercial Road, his father being employed in the Navy Pay Office. The family moved to London two or three years later, and Portsmouth only comes into Dickens' works in *Nicholas Nickleby*, when Nicholas and Smike went there with Vincent Crummles' theatrical company, including the celebrated 'Infant Phenomenon'. The house is now a Dickens Museum, open March to October 10 a.m. to 6 p.m., and November to February 10 a.m. to 4 p.m.

Another Portsmouth-born novelist and poet was George Meredith, born 1828. His grandfather was a tailor, and was the original of 'The Great Mel' in *Evan Harrington*. This novel is, to a certain extent, autobiographical, and so is *The Ordeal of Richard Feverel*, often considered Meredith's best novel. He had rather an unhappy childhood, and an unsuccessful first marriage, and the influence of these is seen in many of his works. He was greatly admired by some readers, and much disliked by others. His style was quite different from that of any previous writer, and some authors considered him too modern at that time. Some modern critics, however, consider him one of our great writers, and he has been compared with D. H. Lawrence.

Portsmouth Harbour. Ferries to Gosport

Sir Arthur Conan Doyle, though not born in Hampshire, practised as a doctor in Portsmouth as a young man, and some of his novels, including *The White Company* and *Micah Clarke* are about Hampshire. One of the famous short stories in *The Adventures of Sherlock Holmes* is 'The Copper Beeches', the action of which takes place in and near Winchester.

Southsea became a very popular seaside resort in Victorian times. It has some handsome houses, a wide common, all the usual seaside pleasures, and the extra attraction of frequent trips to the Isle of Wight, about five miles away. Southsea and Portsmouth suffered very severely in the air-raids of World War II. Many people moved into the villages just inland for the nights, but early every morning, often after only a couple of hours restless sleep in air-raid shelters, they went cheerfully and courageously back into the dockyard or the city to work. Portsmouth Guildhall, a fine Victorian building, was completely destroyed in 1940, but has since been restored in the original style. Many old houses were also destroyed, including the George Hotel in High Street, where Nelson spent his last night ashore. One bomb fell between the *Victory* and the dock wall but, like the spirit of the people, the old ship survived.

The A3 road from Portsmouth to Petersfield runs through some of the most striking Downland in Hampshire. Off the road to the right, about eight miles out of Portsmouth, is Windmill Hill, with the remains of one of Hampshire's few windmills. The first known windmill on this site dated from 1289. In the nearby village of Chalton, there is a beautiful thatched and timbered inn, the Red Lion, believed to be fifteenth century. The Church of St. Michael has an early English chancel with windows with good plate tracery. The east window, *c.* 1270, has four equal lancets with two quatrefoils and one cinquefoil above. Other parts of the church are Decorated, and the font is *c.* 1500.

A mile or so from the village, on Chalton Down, Mr. Budden, a farmer, discovered on his land the site of a very interesting old Saxon settlement, probably dating from the sixth or seventh century. Excavations have revealed, among other things, two rectangular structures with doorways in the middle of the long walls, and sheeps' bones were dug up, showing that sheep-farming, which continued on this part of the Downs until recent times, was already practised at that early date.

Beyond Windmill Hill the road runs through a pass between two of the most impressive Downs, War Down on the east and Butser Hill on the west. The latter is 888 feet high, and one of the highest hills in Hampshire. On its spurs are some earthworks of uncertain date. An Iron Age Camp is being reconstructed there.

Buriton, a pretty little village with a large pond, lies just below War Down, about a mile from the Portsmouth–Petersfield road. The Church of St. Mary has some interesting features of various periods, from the Transition Norman to the eighteenth century. The font is twelfth-century Purbeck marble. The good, early Georgian Manor House was the home of the Gibbons, father and mother of Edward Gibbon the historian. He usually made it his home when he was in England. Between 1760 and 1770, when an invasion by France was considered probable, he and his father both ran detachments of the Hampshire Militia. Edward Gibbon wrote a most entertaining journal of his life at this time, well worth reading by those who might, perhaps, be daunted at undertaking *The Decline and Fall of the Roman Empire*.

Petersfield, about two miles from Buriton, is a pleasant old town. In the Domesday Book it was described as the Manor of Mapledurham, or Mapeldresham, and Buriton was included in this Manor. As late as 1835, Petersfield Church is described as a Chapel of Ease to the Mother Church at Buriton. There are, however, relics of human life at Petersfield from thousands of years before that date. The earliest inhabitants of the district lived on what is now Petersfield Heath, a very popular resort, with a lake and lovely distant views of the Downs. Here was a Mesolithic (Middle Stone Age) site dating from *c.* 5000 B.C. to *c.* 3000 B.C. People of this date occupied places with a sandy soil, with good hunting and the minimum of tree-felling, and on the Heath they had a camp site where have been found very small flint implements, which were probably the barbs and cutting edges of spears.

In about 1600 B.C., there was an invasion of Dorset from Brittany, and this gave rise to the spread of the Wessex Culture, one of the most prominent phases of the Bronze Age. Some time between 1500 B.C. and 1300 B.C., some important people made a settlement in the Petersfield region. This was an immigration of a small body of warrior-chiefs, rather than a full-scale invasion. They proceeded to build up a Bronze Age type of culture, with wide-spreading channels of trade. On Petersfield Heath they have left behind a large necropolis, consisting of different types of barrow. Many are of the usual bowl pattern, but some are of the disc pattern, showing a small mound encircled by a bank, and dating from the Bronze Age. The making of a necropolis here on such a large scale shows that there must have been a tribe or family of considerable importance living in the neighbourhood.

Petersfield Heath

During the last few centuries before the birth of Christ, iron-using people practised agriculture, using small field systems. The Romans, busy with the consolidation of the country, did not disturb their way of life. Once the country was at peace, the well-to-do Romano-British farmer became a part of the picture. A fine example of a Roman villa was found at Stroud, to the west of Petersfield, but was most unfortunately not preserved.

After the departure of the Romans came a dark period of history. Probably dating from this is the great entrenchment at Froxfield, which runs along the top of a ridge about two miles west of Petersfield. It was probably built to defend a gap where there were no trees, or it may have been the boundary between Sussex to the south-east and Wessex to the north-west.

Although, as has been said, in Norman times Petersfield Church was only a Chapel of Ease to Buriton, the town of Petersfield had by this time attained some importance. During the reign of Henry II, the townsmen were granted a Charter by the Duke of Gloucester, giving them all the liberties and free customs enjoyed by the citizens of Winchester. Being childless, Gloucester bequeathed the Manor to the Earl of Moreton, who afterwards became King John who, in 1198, granted a Charter confirming the earlier ones. Throughout the Middle Ages, the town became increasingly important. Leather and cloth manufacture carried on there employed upwards of 1,000 people during the reign of James I, 1603–25.

Statue of William III, The Square, Petersfield

Charles II visited the town. His notorious mistress, the Duchess of Portsmouth, was also created by him Baroness Petersfield and Countess of Fareham.

Petersfield was a Parliamentary borough as far back as 1306–7, but was not represented again until 1522–3. It lost one member by the great Reform Bill of 1832, and the other somewhat later. The Jolliffe family represented the borough almost continuously until 1880, when it was merged into the county, but once during the eighteenth century it was represented by the Hon. William Gerard Hamilton, who created a record. All through his time as a Member of Parliament he made only one speech, but that lasted for fifteen hours. His fellow members knew him as 'Single Speech Hamilton'.

One of the Jolliffe family presented the equestrian statue of William of Orange, dressed as a Roman Emperor. He had no special connection with the town, but Mr. Jolliffe was his great admirer. Formerly in the grounds of the Jolliffe mansion, the statue was later moved to its present position in The Square. It may have been the work of John Cheere, a well-known sculptor of the period.

During the coaching days, Petersfield became a very busy place indeed, lying on the main London–Portsmouth road, but when the railway came, the town was rather deserted. At the turn of the century, however, people began to realise how conveniently the town was situated. Many handsome villas were built, trade looked up, and the coming of the motor-car completed the renaissance of the old town.

St. Peter's Church, in The Square, has an interesting history. When first built, it was a cruciform Norman church with rich central tower, and must have rather resembled East Meon Church. Then, possibly, the tower gave trouble for it was partly taken down, leaving only the east arch of the crossing with three rich Norman windows above. Towards the end of the twelfth century the nave received aisles, thus absorbing the transepts, and a new west tower was built, to which a Perpendicular top was later added. In spite of much knocking about by Victorian restorers, it is still a most interesting and beautiful church. A notable feature is the very striking picture of Christ, standing at the mouth of Fingal's Cave on Staffa, by Gunning King in memory of his wife.

There are still many charming old houses, although some have unfortunately been destroyed. Sheep Street leads out of The Square at its south-west corner. In it is a delightful row of timber-framed houses. This street leads to The Spain, a charming square of old houses, the name commemorating the place where the local wool merchants conducted their business with Spanish woolmen from the continent. One

Sheep Street, Petersfield

of the houses has a tablet stating that John Goodyer, Botanist and Royalist lived there. He made a vast collection of notes, many written on miserable little scraps of paper. He bequeathed his valuable botanical library to Magdalen College, Oxford.

On the corner of The Square and Chapel Street is a fine old timber-framed house with flint nogging. Next door is a very handsome mid-Georgian house, now used by Lloyds Bank. The Punch and Judy Café in High Street is early seventeenth century, and the Red Lion Hotel has a characteristic eighteenth-century front. Dragon House, in the street of the same name, is early eighteenth century, but the back is Elizabethan. The gazebo, a typical eighteenth-century summer house, at the end of the garden, can be seen from the Avenue. In College Street is the fine Georgian house, formerly Churcher's College, but now Council Offices. The cause of education is well served in Petersfield. Churcher's College, now located at the top of Rams-hill on the London Road, was founded in 1722 by Richard Churcher, an East India merchant. In his will he left £3,500 to endow a school for twelve local boys, who were to be taught English, Mathematics and Navigation, and were to be apprenticed to the East India Company. The Victorian buildings at Ramshill are now a Grammar School for boys.

Bedales School, first established at Hayward's Heath in Sussex, was founded in 1893 by J. H. Badley. At first it was a boys' school, but

Stoner Hill near Petersfield

in 1898 girls were admitted, and thus Bedales became the very first co-educational boarding school. In 1900 a move was made to Steep, a short distance to the west of Petersfield, where some excellent modern buildings have been erected.

The Petersfield Musical Festival, first held in 1901, is famous, and has attracted some of the best-known conductors and performers. No visitor to Petersfield should leave without going to Stoner Hill, which lies on the Petersfield–Alresford road. It is one of the most beautiful pieces of scenery in Hampshire, with steep wooded ridges known as 'hangers', of which the Selborne Hanger is the best-known example. At Stoner Hill they form a deep gorge. Near the top of the hill, on the left hand side as one descends, there is a lay-by with a wide view, framed by the gorge, to the east as far as Hindhead, Surrey, eleven miles away. Petersfield is near the Surrey and Sussex borders.

From prehistoric Hengistbury in the west to prehistoric Petersfield in the east; from the trees of the New Forest to the trees of Stoner Hill; from the great docks of Southampton and Portsmouth in the south to the peaceful agricultural country of the north, and with all the history and beauty that lies between, Hampshire is a county without a rival.

Index